SNOWDONIA , WHITE WATER, SEA AND SURF

SNOWDONIA, WHITE WATER, SEA AND SURF

A Canoeing Guide
by Terry Storry

Pont Cyfyng on the River Llugwy.   Photo: Andy Woodhouse

© *Terry Storry 1986*

ISBN 0902363 77 8

First published 1986

About the Author

Terry Storry spent six years at university rock-climbing. On the way he picked up three degrees in history, politics and sociology. After teaching in a comprehensive school for two years, he joined the staff of the National Mountaineering Centre (Plas y Brenin), and as head of rock climbing spent most of his time canoeing. He has canoed in Chile (Rio Bio Bio), North America (Grand Canyon of the Colorado), New Zealand (Buller, Tongariro, Rangitikei, Rangitata, Shotover, Kawarau), and throughout Europe. He is author of 'Alpine White Water' (1982), and co-author of 'North Wales White Water' (1981). He is a British Mountain Guide (U.I.A.G.M.), and a British Canoe Union Senior Instructor, Inland and Sea.

The Author   Photo: Julie Coldwell

Contents

Foreword

Between trips abroad, bouts of idleness, and messing about in boats, this Guide has taken three long years to write. Over that time help has come from too many people to remember or mention. To all those people, thank you.

There are however, a few names that cannot go without mention; Howard Jeffs, who always encouraged when I faltered, and who supplied key information on surf beaches and tidal bores; Nigel Foster, for his Appendix on sea birds and for casting a salty eye over the whole sea guide; Jim Hargreaves, for allowing me to use some material he prepared for 'North Wales White Water'; Andy Sherif, for local knowledge on Dulas Bay and the Swellies; Andy Halliday, Marty Kelly, and Derek Mayes for providing photographs; and last, but not least, Julie Coldwell, who read the whole manuscript, told me when it didn't make sense, and corrected the spelling when it did.

The responsibility for any errors and omissions in the Guide are entirely mine. I have paddled all the substantive trips described, usually more than once, so I should know what I am writing about. If I don't, please contact me; the next edition will be all the better for your pains.

It will be interesting to see the changes in attitude and technique reflected by a second edition. Writing in 1956 Alec Ellis thought Trevor Rocks on the Dee (Grade IIIc), 'a very bad rapid', and recommended that,' when you become really expert you will often be able to stand up in the canoe and inspect an approaching rapid'. In the same 'Book of Canoeing' he has the following advice for sea canoeists; 'if a landing has to be made on a rockbound shore, jump out and swim for it when well away from the surf'. I expect the next thirty years will make present standards look equally dated. Fortunately, water is not aged, nor staled, by custom.

T.S.
Plas y Brenin
Christmas 1985

Introduction

There is nothing, to paraphrase Rat in 'The Wind in the Willows', absolutely nothing half so much worth doing as simply messing about in boats in Snowdonia. Here is a mountain range on the edge of the sea, the rivers falling three thousand feet in a day's walk, the sea, and surf, funnelled and accelerated by deep bays, huge cliffs, and jutting headlands, and all around slate and limestone, kestrel and puffin, parsley fern and spleenwort.

The area covered by the Guide stretches from Bardsey Island in the west, to Llangollen in the east, from the Skerries in the north, to Dolgellau in the south. It is a selective Guide, the best of river, sea, and surf 'canoeing' (used as a generic term for canoeing, kayaking, and skiing) in North Wales. The Guide is written in the form of trip descriptions, except for the Surf Guide. There are sixteen rivers, fourteen sea trips, twelve surf beaches, and two tidal bores, some familiar to remember and repeat, but many new to follow and find out about. All are within a day's drive of each other.

Most river rats will have paddled the Tryweryn and the Dee, many will know the Llugwy, Ogwen, and Conwy, but the Wnion, Colwyn, Seiont and Mawddach, are not as popular as they deserve to be. Many sea dogs will have been round the Stacks, out to the Skerries and to Bardsey. These are the great classics of the area; but how many know their way round Holy Island or the Tudwals, and who has been in the underground passages beneath Trwyn-y-Tal? Skis and shoes do battle with boards at Hell's Mouth and Cable Bay, but where do surfers go when a fresh wind blows from the north or east?

Since I co-authored 'North Wales White Water' five years ago, improved technique, better training, and great advances in boat design, have altered the face of canoeing in North Wales. This has been most obvious in river canoeing. Fresh rapids and rivers are canoed every month - the best are here in the Guide - and in the new plastic boats, Grade VI is no longer thought suicidal or expensive. And recently another branch of river running has become popular on the harder rivers - rafting.

Partly to cope with the increasing standards in wild water canoeing, I have introduced a new grading system, as well as using Grade VI for the first time. Grading is a subject which provokes much debate, and no doubt those used in this Guide will be no exception. I have tried to grade rivers as they would appear to someone paddling them for the first time, and avoid the downgrading game common amongst high

7

achievers (in every sport).

Rising standards in sea canoeing are less obvious, but no less real. Specialist sea kayaks are now a common sight round Anglesey, open sea crossings of more than thirty kilometres not unusual, and the only limitation on really long crossings is the inability to sleep in a kayak. The great range of trips now open to the load-carrying, straight-running sea canoeist, suggested the possibility of grading - according to distance from land, ease of landing, tidal influence and so on. In the end however, I decided that, on the sea, the weather introduces too many changes to make grading very useful.

If sea paddlers are quietly pushing back the frontiers, surf canoeists have, in the last five years, ridden a crashing wave of change. Shoes are out, kayaks are just for fun, it is the age of the Ski. And like the product from which it borrows the name, there is a new one every year, faster, or more manoeuvrable, or better looking, than the one before.

I am sure the *next* five and twenty years will continue to see radical change in sport. I am equally sure that it will be the same rivers, the same coastline, and the same beaches that are being paddled. They will only be worth visiting however, if they have not been destroyed. Guidebooks are sometimes criticised for encouraging over-use of fragile natural environments. I do feel the sense of this criticism, and believe canoeists have to make agreements amongst themselves, and with other interested parties - bird watchers, anglers, sailboarders, surfers, landowners - to restrict access to use. These restrictions however, are only good when openly agreed between interested parties. They are not good when based on elitist arguments, or unequal divisions of power. A guide merely presents the possibilities. It is up to the users to come to fair agreements about the when and where.

Guidebooks are also criticised for removing the adventure and excitement involved in personal discovery. This applies less to canoeing guides than climbing guides; water, unlike rock, is malleable, so conditions on the day will always require personal interpretation and judgement. It applies even less to a selective canoeing guide such as this.

There is much to do in North Wales that is not in these pages. For instance, parts of all the following rivers have been paddled: The Nantperis below Cromlech Bridge in the Llanberis Pass; the Caseg foaming into Bethesda out of the Carneddau; the Llan cascading down beside the Watkin Path from Snowdon; the Goch, a short hard section behind the Snowdon Railway Station in Llanberis; the dam controlled

Alwen, flowing into the Dee out of the Denbigh Moors; the Goedol running out of Tan-y-grisiau, near Blaenau Ffestiniog, over a number of very big drops; the mild-mannered Gallen flowing beside the A.548 near Llangernyaw; the Dwyfor out of Cwm Pennant and to the sea at Criccieth; and finally, the Wen falling steeply into the lower Mawddach. So there is plenty to keep 'gold diggers' happy. And there must be many rivers still to be discovered, particularly in the outlying areas of the Denbigh Moors, Nantle Ridge, Rhinogs and Arenigs.

Similarly the possibilities for sea canoeing are by no means limited to the areas mentioned in this Guide, let alone to the particular trips described. For example, between Barmouth and Pwllheli there is much of interest to explore, including Sarn Badrigg, or St. Patrick's Causeway, a fifteen kilometre strip of rock and sand exposed at low water. And even on the trips described, there are dozens of small rips and swirling eddies, a hundred little barnacled bays and gullies, and a thousand cormorant covered crags and skerries, which have gone unremarked, and yet are remarkable. So the Guide will start you on the way, but the rest is out there for you to find.

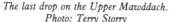

The last drop on the Upper Mawddach.
Photo: Terry Storry

Wild water - the Llugwy.   Photo:Stewart Brooks

THE
RIVER GUIDE

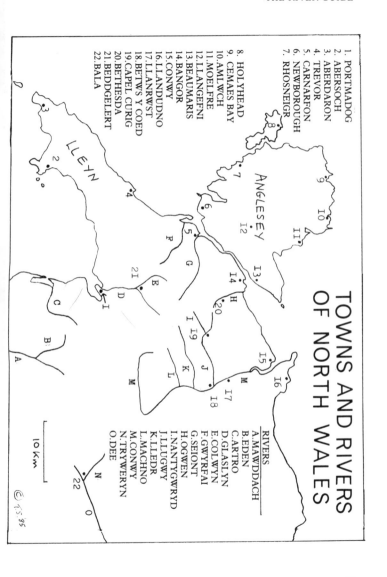

TOWNS AND RIVERS OF NORTH WALES

1. PORTMADOG
2. ABERSOCH
3. ABERDARON
4. TREVOR
5. CARNARFON
6. NEWBOROUGH
7. RHOSNEIGR
8. HOLYHEAD
9. CEMAES BAY
10. AMLWCH
11. MOELFRE
12. LLANGEFNI
13. BEAUMARIS
14. BANGOR
15. CONWY
16. LLANDUDNO
17. LLANRWST
18. BETWS Y COED
19. CAPEL CURIG
20. BETHESDA
21. BEDDGELERT
22. BALA

RIVERS
A. MAWDDACH
B. EDEN
C. ARTRO
D. GLASLYN
E. COLWYN
F. GWYRFAI
G. SEIONT
H. OGWEN
I. NANTYGWRYD
J. LLUGWY
K. LLEDR
L. MACHNO
M. CONWY
N. TRYWERYN
O. DEE

10 km

© 15.85

River Canoeing and the Guide

Most rivers in this Guide are not described in their entirety. This is not because other sections of the rivers cannot be paddled, but because these others parts are considered either too tiresome because of the number of portages required, or too tedious because of the lack of white water. Even in the sections described, there will be gaps. An eddy by eddy description is neither possible nor desirable. Every portage and significant fall is mentioned and mapped, but the canoeist will often have to discover for himself the intricacies of the river in between.

There is another factor which should impress caution on all canoeists using the Guidebook. Rivers change through the intervention of man, in the shape of weirs, fences, and channelling, and through the intervention of nature, in the shape of fallen trees, floods, and droughts. In other words, in time some of the descriptions may become inaccurate. It is always worth checking with local paddlers for up-to-date knowledge.

River Levels

The most crucial factor that the canoeist will have to take into account when using the Guide, is the level of the river. These descriptions take it as given that the rivers are being canoed just *off the flood*. This means that the river is as high as it can be while still flowing between its normal banks.

Apart from the Tryweryn, which is dam controlled, and the Dee, which is a 'mature' river, the rivers in this Guide depend on rainfall to make them canoeable. A good rough guide to the amount of water in the rivers, is the state of the mountain streams in the Ogwen, Llanberis, and Gwynant valleys. If these streams, which are easily seen on the bare moorland slopes, are white the rivers will probably be 'up'.

Some rivers stay up longer than others. The Llugwy and Lledr hold their water well, the Conwy best of all, but most of the other rivers have weak bladders. Local canoeists use various measures to judge levels. For the Llugwy there is a height gauge below Plas Y Brenin where the fence leads into the slalom pool - 2-4: minimum level for canoeing; 6-8: off the flood as described in this Guide; 10+: over the banks and Cobdens is Vd. For the Seiont there is a shingle bed at Pont Rhythallt which is submerged when the river is up. On the Conwy, a small rapid below Bryn Bras Falls, and visible, on the drive up the A.5., should be well covered. If the gauge by the bridge above the

Warws reads 4 or 5, the Colwyn - and the Aberglaslyn Gorge - are in good condition.

No doubt a marker could be devised for each river in the Guide. *But* such markers are hard to find, unreliable in use - for instance, the gauge at Plas y Brenin is on the Nantygwryd, and so does not take into account water coming down the Upper Llugwy - and only have 'meaning' to locals, who know the rivers anyway. For these reasons I do not put much reliance on river level markers, and have largely ignored them in this Guide.

Suffice it to say that canoeing on these 'young' rivers changes, sometimes dramatically, with the water level. Generally, the higher the rate of flow, the harder and more serious the water. The difference between high and low volume can be as much as a Grade. The canoeist therefore, will have to, and, of course, will want to make his own judgement about the level of the river on the day. Sometimes a bottom-scraper is better than nothing; at other times, the jaded paddler will only put in when the rivers are brown.

Descriptions

The river descriptions in this Guide are in geographical clockwise order round North Wales. Each description is followed by a map of the river, except in the case of the Colwyn, Nantmor, and Nantygwryd. Maps of the former two are included with the Glaslyn, and the latter may be found with the Llugwy.

The terms left and right in the descriptions refer to the 'true' left and right banks of the river - that is looking in the direction of flow, or downstream. The terms above/before and below/after also relate to the direction of flow, meaning, in other words, upstream and downstream.

Most landmarks have a six figure grid reference. This is accurate to the nearest one hundred metres and is taken from the appropriate 1:50,000 Ordnance Survey Map of the area. The map title and sheet number of all these maps is given in Appendix VI. The grid references are to be preferred for accuracy to the marked features on the Guide-book maps.

Maps

The Guidebook maps have been drawn with the river bank reader in mind. They are a quick visual guide to the river giving only the essential information. Portages have been marked with a P and the following symbol ⌐⌐ , and major *individual* falls are named and marked thus ◠ . All falls which have not been canoed are marked

13

as portages, as well as a few horror stories that have been canoed.

The maps are drawn to scale (1:50,000), but they are drawn by hand, so the distance between features, and the prominence of features, cannot be relied upon for absolute accuracy. Indeed some features, such as towns, have been deliberately minimised, whilst others, such as rivers and roads, have been maximised. And a good deal of information, not directly relevant to the canoeist, has been omitted altogether. For instance, only those roads directly impinging on the rivers are shown on the maps. All this is to make the maps easier for the canoeist to use.

Access

As I write these lines, two related trends in our times, are forcing the issue of access to the forefront. The first is unemployment, now worse than at any time during the Great Depression. The second is the steady growth of canoeing - there are now over 100,000 people doing 'it' - putting increased pressure on water use. And just as the battle of the grouse moors in the 1930's, between landowners and ramblers, drew people from the workless northern cities, so, today, the cold war on the rivers is catching fire, as landowners try to protect their natural assets from the popular demand for more ways to spend 'free' time.

Pity it is that we had no social revolution. We did our best in 1649, but it was not enough. We have no precedents for, say, the Swedish solution, where an 'Everymans Law' allows all Swedish citizens to cross land or water (public or private) for the purposes of recreation, providing they do not cause damage or harm (for which they will be held responsible).

So we must muddle through with the weight of antiquated property rights around our shoulders. A start has been made at the Tryweryn, where canoeists have bought access rights, and now pay for 'it'. Whether anyone should ever have to pay for 'it' is open to question, but it may be the price for guaranteed access and parking/camping/ changing facilities. Another obvious solution for wild water rivers is an agreement based around the fishing season (see Appendix V), for these rivers are usually best for canoeing outside the fishing season. Yet again there might be an agreement based on water levels -canoeing allowed when the river is in spate as defined by a gauge -, or days of the week, or certain times of the day. At the time of writing there are no such agreements in force for rivers in this Guide, except for the Tryweryn and the Dee (races, race training, and open days). Other rivers can only be paddled, therefore, by canoeists willing to accept the possibility of complaints of trespass.

The British Canoe Union, and all local canoeists, deplore this state of affairs, but cannot condone, advise, incite, or encourage trespass. Nevertheless, where no access agreements are in force, B.C.U. disciplinary procedures do not permit any action to be taken against members who venture onto 'private' water without permission, and apart from warning them of the risk of legal action, nothing can be done to restrain them.

All disputes should be referred to the Regional Access Officer of the British Canoe Union. He should also be sought for details of any changes in water use agreements. Members, clubs, and centres, should not ask for special arrangements, as this only makes it more difficult for the access officer to make proper agreements.

Canoeists wish to enjoy their sport, so we must respect the desire of fishermen to enjoy theirs. Whenever there are people fishing, canoeists should pass by quietly on the other side, and not 'play' on the river. This is part of the canoeists code of conduct, and makes us good ambassadors for the sport.

If you decide to paddle on waters where there are no access agreements, be sure to get on and take off by a public right of way (most footpaths and bridges), or, if in doubt, ask the landowner's permission. It must be emphasised that mention of access and egress in this Guide, is no evidence of the right to put on or land from the river. Nor should anything written here be construed as advice or encouragement to trespass.

The next twenty years will surely see many access problems sorted. We now know that a right of navigation exists on some rivers either from 'time immemorial', or from regular use over a period of twenty years or more. Even where legal rights are non-existent, there is a good moral case for water use by every person. Most individual fishermen agree with us. After all they, or their children, or their children's children, will also like messing about in boats. Looked at in this way there is no conflict of interest in opening up all our rivers.

River Grading

Introduction

All the rivers in this guide, with the exception of the Dee, are young rivers. Typically, therefore, they turn sharply, fall suddenly and are strewn with boulders. This makes the water highly technical to paddle. Many of the small rivers in this guide therefore, have a relatively high technical grading.

Apart from the difficulty of the canoeing however, there are two major hazards which should be mentioned. One danger particularly associated with young rivers flowing through wooded country, is their tendency to overflow their banks in flood, causing the current to set through trees, bushes and branches. In low water fallen trees can occasionally block the entire river. The author has witnessed major epics with canoeists trapped upside down in their boats against trees.

A second lethal danger is the advent along the way of unsuspected waterfalls, and weirs. A number of people every year do falls that they had no intention of doing, and although no-one has yet swam Swallow or Conwy Falls, both Horseshoe and Llangollen Town weirs have had inexperienced canoeists nearly drowned. The moral is clear; use this guide and the grading as an aid, but *always* inspect what lies ahead before you paddle it.

A new grading system

Canoeists have, for a long time, shunned anything like the rock climber's detailed and precise grading system. There were good reasons for this. River grading is a much more imprecise art, because the subject matter is malleable. Like the grading used in snow and ice climbing, but unlike that used in rock climbing, it must be broad enough to cope with different conditions. The amount of rain, and in Alpine areas the degree of snow melt, affects the difficulty and seriousness of rivers. To classify rivers therefore, there were just six grades, each grade covering a wide spread of technical difficulty and potential danger.

The problem with this system is that it has been impossible to adequately grade easy, but dangerous, rivers or rapids, and conversely hard, but safe, rivers or rapids. Usually the factors which make manoeuvres hard, also make for frightening water, and normally a rapid which only requires a few paddle strokes will not worry those doing breast stroke. But, and this is an important but, there are many exceptions. Consider Horseshoe Falls which is technically Grade III, but in terms of commitment, is Grade V; many weirs will fall into that category. Then there is the top section of the Tryweryn which is Grade IV in terms of difficulty, but is Grade III for seriousness. The Tombstones on the Dee, is Grade III for canoeing, but dangerous, therefore IV. Pont y Pair on the Llugwy is desperately committing (VI), but the line is fairly obvious (V); and so on.

So we need to separate difficulty from danger, and yet retain a simple and, of necessity, broad grading system. What I have done in the guide, is to classify difficulty according to the traditional grades of I to VI, and to classify danger by using the letters a to f. I am convinced this will help the river canoeists decide what he can do, *and* what he wants to do. I hope it will set a pattern for the future.

The new grading system is defined below. At the present time Grade VI and Grade f are the upper limits. It is not, however, a closed system, and as standards of equipment and canoeing continue to rise, so new numbers and letters can be added to the system. Grade VII and Grade g will not be long in the making.

Bryn Bras Falls on Conwy Upper Gorge.
Photo: Terry Storry

17

Alphabetical grades of seriousness

a. Safe.

There are no obstructions in the river. It is always possible to swim to the bank with a boat.

b. Little Danger.

The occasional rock, overhanging branch, or bridge pillar, can cause problems, but rescue is simple and quick. Swimming to the bank is no problem, but a boat may have to be shunted.

c. Some Danger.

Obstructions can pin or jam a boat, but a long and bumpy swim will hurt the pride more than the body. Ropes and lines are sometimes useful in rescues. An Eskimo roll can save problems.

d. Dangerous.

The force of water can trap canoe and canoeist against obstacles. Stoppers may hold boats, but not swimmers. A swim is usually unpleasant and occasionally injurious, so the ability to roll is important. Rescues from the bank may be necessary.

e. Very Dangerous.

Rescues from circulating stoppers, boulder chokes, jammed logs, and sumps, are all very difficult. There is little another person in a boat can do to help; prepared bank security is normal. A swim is dangerous, so rolling is essential. There are committing ravines or gorges.

f. Extremely Dangerous.

Mistakes may be dearly payed for; there is a definite danger to life and limb. Luck is more likely than rescue to be a saviour. Rolling is problematical in the turbulent water. Evacuation from the river will be difficult. Modern safety equipment in the canoeist's gear, and the specialised wild water boat, will improve the paddler's chances of winning.

Numerical grades of technical difficulty.

I. Easy.

Here are rivers with beautiful united waters, flowing in peaceful meanders down laughing valleys. The canoe may float any way which it pleases down the channel.

II. Moderate.

The river is already quicker. At moments there is a disturbance which the canoe sails over with disdain. An overhanging tree forces the canoeist into some adriot steering. A rock in the main channel must be avoided. But always the channel is clear and obvious.

III. *Fairly Difficult.*

Now things are more complicated. The current is swift. Sometimes the river becomes narrow with big waves. The canoeist may have to manoeuvre between rocks, stop in eddies, and cross currents. Nevertheless the best channel is easily recognized and remembered.

IV. *Difficult.*

This is challenging water. Rapids follow each other in quick succession, or are continuous and difficult to read. Cushion waves build on obstacles and stoppers form below constrictions. The route is not obvious from the water, so inspection from the bank will be necessary to remember the way.

V. *Very Difficult.*

Even after inspection from the bank, it is often difficult to recognize a route through Grade V water. There are pressure waves, whirlpools, boils, waterfalls and holding stoppers. The water is always fast, often heavy, and the eddies are very sharp. A steep gradient, tight bends, and large boulders will hide the river from the canoeist on the water.

VI. *Extremely Difficult.*

All previously mentioned difficulties are increased to (the present) limit of possibility, Grade VI water is a playing field of descents and foaming chaos. To all but the most experienced, and inexperienced, canoeist the river will appear impossible. It is runnable only at particular water levels. The paddler can expect at times to disappear completely, and at others to be hurled skywards by a prodigious force. The water sucks and surges unpredictably, often making route choice academic. Reactive skills must be of the highest order.

Notes:

1) Whenever a rapid or river is graded, the technical grading comes first, followed by the grading for seriousness, as in, for example, The Serpents Tail (IVc). This is because most people are already familiar with the numerical grades, and can at first, relate to them in isolation. Secondly, most people like to find out whether they *can* do a rapid, before they find out what might happen if they can't.

2) The descriptions are intentially vague and general to cope with a wide variety of rapid types and water conditions. Flood conditions however, may alter (usually raise) the grade of a river or rapid. Rivers are graded for when they are just *off* the flood, that is when they are as high as they can be while still flowing between their normal banks.

3) I have drawn on a French description of the International Grading System for some of the technical grades of difficulty. A full translation of this is given in my 'Alpine White Water' Guide.

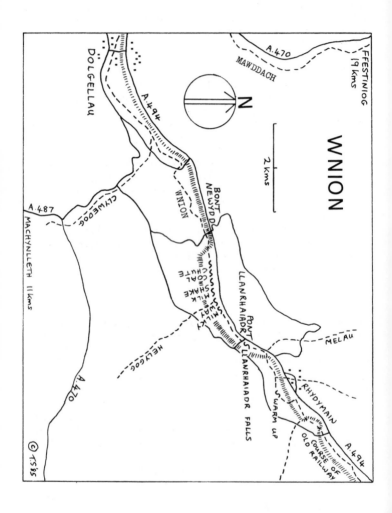

The Wnion

Difficulty: Grade IVd
Access: Bridge 2 kilometres above Rhydymain (G.R.807229)
Egress: Bont Newydd (G.R.770201)
Length: 6 kilometres

Introduction

I first heard of the Wnion in October 1985 shortly after finishing this Guide. A local canoeist wrote singing its praises, and two weeks later, after a day of heavy rain, I was able to confirm his view - and finish what he had started. His tantalising letter was an introduction to the river I found impossible to resist - may it also be for you; it will be worth it.

'...We stopped just before a left-hand bend in this section to inspect what lay beyond. What we came across amazed us - a long gorge with virtually continuous white water with grade IV falls one after the other. The water was belting through very very quickly. The most impressive thing, though, was the length of it, since we walked downstream for at least three-quarters of a mile, but still it carried on! We've no idea what lies beyond this point, because, needless to say, we bottled out of paddling the gorge....'

The River

The main road between Bala and Dolgellau (A.494) runs along the right bank of the Wnion as the river descends to the estuary of the Mawddach. On the section described here, the track of a disused railway parallels the bank for most of the way, crossing to the right on occasions. Both road and railway provide a handy means of prior inspection.

A road leading south off the A.494 less that two kilometres upstream of Rhydymain crosses the river and marks the access point. A small lay-by above the bridge on the right bank leads to the river. Above, the Wnion is little more than a stream, and of no interest to the white water canoeist.

The river, small at first, is soon swollen by tributaries from north and south. It passes under the railway four times before Pont Llanrhaiadr, and the last of these bridges is partially blocked by a tree. The canoeing is continuous and enjoyable at Grade IIb, except for a tiny gorge just after the third bridge - *Warm Up* (IIIb).

Pont Llanrhaiadr (G.R.795209), a roadbridge, marks the half-way point and the start of more difficult canoeing. *Llanrhaiadr Falls* (IIIb) is a one drop wonder just before the bridge, occasionally providing spectacular back-enders. Below the canoeing is fairly continuous Grade IIIb for a kilometre, until the river visibly drops away on a left-hand bend. This is the start of a harder kilometre of water (Grade IVc) in an ever narrowing gorge.

The gorge is divided into two distinct sections, both about half a kilometre in length. The first section has open and relatively accessible banks. It begins steeply at the afore-mentioned left-hand bend, and continues falling, with holes and haystacks forming, as it turns back to the right. This is *Milky Way* a superb bouncy ride. A short flatter interlude interposes, before *Milk Shake* a two tier drop leading to a huge eddy on the left. The last fall in this first section - *Vinegar Stroke* - is partially hidden from the river, but holds no unpleasant surprises. The canoeing throughout is top quality, difficult but not serious (IVc), and reminiscent of the Alps.

The second section of the gorge - *The Coal Chute* (IVd) - follows after a hundred metres. It is a long, very narrow, fast funnel of water bounded by twenty foot sheer rock walls. This is not the place to meet a fallen tree - at the time of writing there is one near the top easily avoided - because there is no escape except to paddle, or be flushed, out the bottom. But as long as the last storm has left no debris, The Coal Chute is relatively safe, being free of stoppers and undercuts. So the excitement here is more like the fun of the fair than the feel of battle, inconsequential thrills and spills rather than the grim surge of flight or fright. Unlike many horror shows, it is as enjoyable in the doing as in the telling, and you will want another ride.

After The Coal Chute the river relaxes, under the railway again, and for half a kilometre to Bont Newydd. Egress is below Newydd Bridge on the left bank. It is possible to continue for another six kilometres to Dolgellau, on quiet and placid water amidst the verdant greenery of Welsh Wales. But those with white water wanderlust will prefer to drive ten kilometres north to add the Eden and Mawddach to a rip snorting day on the right stuff. Good times paddle driver.

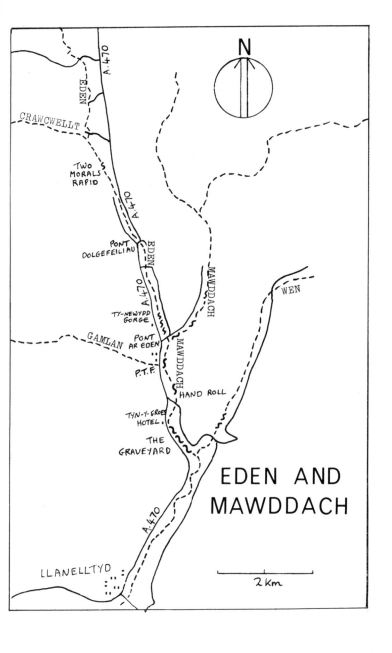

N

EDEN

A.470

CRAWCWELLT

TWO MORALS RAPID

A.470

PONT DOLGEFEILIAU

EDEN

A.470

MAWDDACH

WEN

TY-NEWYDD GORGE

GAMLAN

PONT AR EDEN

P.T.F.

MAWDDACH

HAND ROLL

TYN-Y-GROES HOTEL

THE GRAVEYARD

EDEN AND MAWDDACH

A.470

LLANELLTYD

2 km

The Eden/Mawddach

Difficulty: Eden Grade IIIc; Mawddach Grade IVd.
Access: Pont y Grible (G.R.708304); Pont Dolgefeiliau
(G.R.720269).
Egress: Pont ar Eden (G.R.727248); Effluent of Wen
(G.R.733224).
Length: 10 kilometres

Introduction

The Eden and Mawddach taken together provide a classic white water run. The Eden is very continuous at the grade, and the Lower Mawddach can provide the largest volume of white water of any river in the Guide. There are no portages to interrupt the trip, and the Coed y Brenin forest provides a splendid sense of isolation from the neighbouring roads, not to mention shelter from the disagreeable weather in which the rivers must often be paddled.

The Upper Eden is usually only possible while it is still raining, and the Lower Eden and Mawddach should not be left too long after a storm. The rivers rise and fall like a cistern, because the sea is only ten kilometres downstream. So this is a good place to be when other rivers are too high. Then the Rhinogs and Arenigs will be streaming, the Eden becomes a superb and yet still 'easy' helter skelter, and the Mawddach thunders brown down its motorway.

In the unlikely event that you become bored with the Eden/Mawddach, it is worth considering two other river trips in the area, the *Upper* Mawddach and the Wen. The Upper Mawddach is best canoed from the confluence with the Gain (G.R.735273), reached by a forestry track on the left bank, to the confluence with the Eden. The river varies in difficulty over its length and according to water level, and has a number of technical and serious drops. If these are portaged the Upper Mawddach can be paddled at IVd; medium to low water is preferred. The Wen is somewhat easier (IIId), but has a very difficult, probably uncanoed section just before it enters the Mawddach. A road leads four kilometres up the left bank to the access bridge (G.R.750256). High water is necessary to make this small tributary canoeable. Fallen trees will force the occasional portage.

UPPER EDEN -
PONT Y GRIBBLE TO PONT DOLGEFEILIAU
Grade IIIc; 5 Kilometres
The recently strengthened bridge at Pont y Grible is reached from the
A.470 by a poorly marked and gated no through road. Access is
straightforward, but may not be so for long, since there are plans to
extend Llyn Trawsfyndd and build a second nuclear power station.
Two alternative, although less accessible, put-in's are available
through farms after one and two kilometres.

From these lower access points you will miss little except a string of
barbed wire across the river after half a kilometre, and several small
rapids (IIb). After two kilometres a bridge (access), and a major
tributary entering from the right (the Crawcwellt), heralds the start of
more interesting water as the river enters Coed y Brenin forest.

Two Morals rapid - named during a solo descent of this section when
my canoe was blown into the river as I was inspecting the rapid - is
preceded by a weir with a large black box water gauge on the left. This
is obvious from above, but *Two Morals* is difficult to read from the
river. Below the Eden becomes wilder and is strewn with boulders,
providing interesting canoeing in flood, but a frustrating blunder and
bash in anything less. A good test of the level is the island rapid just
above Pont Dolgefeiliau. If this looks bony, then it is best to leave the
Upper Eden to another day.

LOWER EDEN -
PONT DOLGEFEILIAU TO PONT AR EDEN
Grade IIIc; 2 Kilometres
At Pont Dolgefeiliau the main road (A.470) crosses the river from the
left to right bank, and remains on that side of the Eden (and of the
Mawddach as far as Llanelltyd). The Eden is still wide and rocky after
the bridge, but the water is somewhat more channelled than above. A
forestry road bridge soon appears (unmarked on the 1:50,000 O.S.
map), and a little way further a broken weir forms a pronounced drop.

After one kilometre an old stone barn on the left, and some houses
high on the right, herald the beginnings of Ty-newydd Gorge. The
gorge is neither steep, deep, nor particularly imposing, but there is a
distinct narrowing of the river with some quite exciting drops (IIIc).
The gorge is narrow enough to be blocked by large trees on occasions.
The last rapid is just before Pont ar Eden, and egress is below the
bridge on the left. Most, however, will want to continue over a small
weir and on into the Lower Mawddach.

LOWER MAWDDACH -
CONFLUENCE WITH EDEN TO EFFLUENT OF WEN
Grade IVd; 3 Kilometres

The emerald waters of the Eden are soon muddied by the murky Mawddach, as, soon after the confluence, the two rivers churn together over a big weir. Ganllwyd Weir should be shot in the middle or on the right, and can form a powerful stopper in flood. Not far below is *Public Toilet Falls*, named after the local conveniences in Ganllwyd - convenient indeed for some paddlers after they have inspected the rapid! P.T.F. or S.H.F. is a severe narrowing of the river containing an enormous boulder (IVd). In low water the boulder is visible, in medium water it forms a large stopper, and in high water it is hidden beneath a huge brown wave. A route to the left of the boulder seems best in most conditions.

Below P.T.F. a footbridge is followed by a smaller rapid and the Afon Gamlan pouring in from the right. Three hundred metres downstream is *Hand Roll* (IIIc), a fairly innocuous drop on a left hand bend. Smaller rapids follow, and then a roadbridge. Below is Tyn-y-groes bend, with the hotel of the same name high above the retaining wall on the right. This marks the start of *The Graveyard*, a superb kilometre of boulder filled rapids (IIIc), or, in high water, powerful stoppers and holes (IVd). This is the best of the Mawddach, and in flood can provide very heavy water.

The last rapids of The Graveyard peter out above an obvious right hand bend. The remaining five kilometres above Llanelltyd are Grade Ia, so the white water canoeist will want to take out here. Just above the effluent of the Wen flowing in from the left, a footpath leads up to the back road. This in turn will take the canoeist back to the A.470 by the bridge above Tyn-y-groes bend.

The Artro

Difficulty: Grade IIIc
Access: Lay-by (G.R.621298); or Pen-y-Bont (G.R.607281)
Egress: Llanbedr (G.R.585268)
Length: 5 kilometres or 2 kilometres

Introduction

Mischievously dubbed 'The Raging River of the Rhinogs', the Artro *is* surprisingly fast for such a small river. It starts gently enough through wooded slopes and hedged fields, but then drops steeply through a narrow gorge.

The Artro runs out of Cwm Bychan, draining the Western Rhinogs in it's haste to reach Cardigan Bay near Llanbedr. It is approached from Harlech in the north, or Barmouth to the south. A short, narrow river, it runs off extremely quickly and can only be paddled after torrential rain. It is best to launch while the downpour is still in progress. When full to the brim, it is preferable to put-in at Pen-y-Bont as low trees make the top section tiresome and somewhat dangerous. At lower levels the upper stretch provides a good warm-up, although care is still required.

Should the Artro be in flood, it is fairly safe to assume that so are the Eden and Mawddach, since they are on the other side of the catchment area. This being the case there is an excellent day's paddling to be had on these three rivers.

The River

The road from Llanbedr follows the right bank of the Artro up into Cwm Bychan. Before reaching the Cwm, two parking spots next to the river offer a choice of access points. The top one, next to a small stone bridge (above Crafnant), is most convenient. From here, three kilometres of Grade IIc leads down to the third bridge at Pen-y-Bont. Campsites litter the left bank, and fallen trees and low slung branches litter the river. The water however, is slow and easy to read.

The bridge at Pen-y-Bont marks the start of a kilometre of Grade IIIc through a small and scenic gorge. The first section of rapids are the hardest on the river, with one notable fall burying you in the stopper below. The junction with the Afon Cwmnanteol, just below the fourth stone bridge, marks the end of the difficulties, and it is possible to get out just above the bridge, on the left bank, by some houses. Alternatively continue down to Llanbedr, where another bridge (the fifth) marks the egress point.

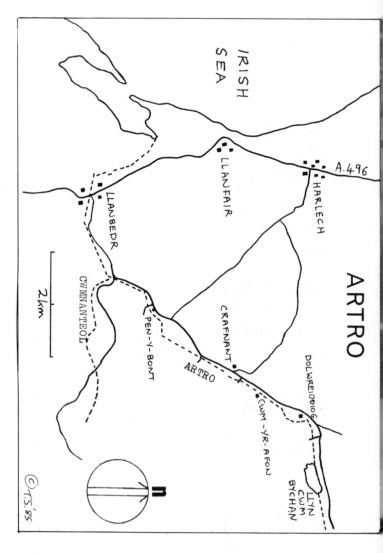

The Glaslyn

Difficulty: Sections of Grade IIc, and Vd
Access: Llyn Dinas (G.R.613413); Lay-by (G.R.593468)
Egress: Lay-by (G.R. as above); Pont Aber Glaslyn (G.R.594461)
Length: 5 kilometres

Introduction

Looking towards Beddgelert from the 'pass' of Aberglaslyn - the Aberglaslyn Gorge - George Borrow, the romantic author of 'Wild Wales', was eloquent in his description.

> 'Before me lay the meadow of Gelert with the river flowing through it towards the pass. Beyond the meadow the Snowdon range; on the right the mighty Cerrig Llan; on the left, the equally mighty, but not quite so precipitous, Hebog. Truly the valley of Gelert is a wondrous valley - rivalling for grandeur and beauty any vale either in the Alps or the Pyrenees.'

What luck then, to find a river running through this valley, fast and powerful in flood, with white water easy enough at the start to relax amidst the scenery, and hard enough at the finish to satisfy the most jaded adrenalin junkie.

The river Glaslyn may be divided into three distinct sections. There are the reclaimed estuarial flats of the lower Glaslyn below Aberglaslyn bridge, described by the B.C.U. Waterways Guide as the only 'practicable' section of the river (Grade Ia). There is the gorge of the Glaslyn, immediately above the bridge, one of the hardest bits of water in North Wales (Grade Vc), and the scene of many epics. And there is the upper Glaslyn running from Llyn Dinas to the top of the gorge, through hill country so well described by Borrow (Grade IIb).

THE UPPER GLASLYN

Grade IIb; 4 kilometres

From the Upper Glaslyn it is best to put in at the lower of the two lakes in the Gwynant valley, Llyn Dinas. There are convenient parking places on the A.498 lake shore road. A short paddle on the lake leads south-west into the river past an old boat-house. Between the lake and Beddgelert, the river twists and turns through beautiful hill country, Snowdon to the west and the Moelwyns to the east. Two road bridges are passed on this section, before another two bridges close together and in the village of Beddgelert, appear round the corner. Here the river is grade IIb for a hundred yards as it is at once

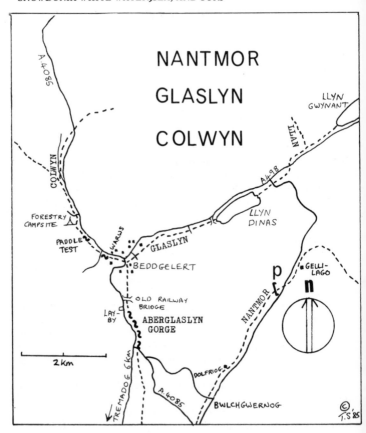

constricted by bridge arches, and accelerated by a series of drops (G.R.591480).

At the bottom of *Gelert's rapid*, do not turn right or you will be canoeing the Afon Colwyn upstream! The upper Glaslyn continues for another kilometre, rather bigger, but no harder (IIb), for the addition of the Colwyn. A footbridge and the re-appearance of the A.498 road next to the river gives you plenty of warning of the approaching gorge (G.R.591473). A series of small drops with big pools below, are a good note on which to end the trip - there is a convenient lay-by on the other side of the road. Beware, however, of going one drop too far, unless of course your aim is to do the gorge; the gorge may end up 'doing' you.

THE ABERGLASLYN GORGE
Grade Vd; 1 kilometre

A few meanders south of Beddgelert the Glaslyn starts it's break from the mountains to the sea. It carves a way through in just a kilometre, hardly more than a minute's drive by road. But one look at the Aberglaslyn Gorge in flood will remind hardened alpinists how much excitement there is to be had in a kilometre of water. So peek shyly over the wall if you will, or gaze hesitantly from the bridge at the bottom, or inspect brazenly from the cat walk on the left bank, and imagine yourself there. You will join many others who have....and who have left it for another day.

Access to the Gorge is from a lay-by on the neighbouring A.498 two hundred metres above and on the right. The water at the get-in should cover all the rocks and shelves if the Gorge below is to be in good nick. The start of the Gorge is marked by a narrowing of the rocks walls, and the water immediately falls steeply between large boulders. The odd break-out is possible, and helpful to rehearse the next moves, for the route is hard to remember. This and the hard section below can be easily inspected from the path on the left bank.

The Gorge now broadens out and there is a notable fall on the right -a double drop in low water. This fall is called *The Breaker* because of the damage it has done over the years; it carries a powerful stopper. The Breaker is invisible from the road being tucked under the high retaining wall, a position which makes it hard to protect from the bank.

Below The Breaker, the Gorge is still hard, but the best, or worst, is now over. There is continuous white water to the bridge, and then....nothing, except more placid meanders, the Glaslyn's fluid ounces of energy seemingly all spent in the turmoil above. Egress can be made immediately below the bridge on the left, but to relax with the river it is best to float further down, and scramble to the road on the right. Should it be misty, it is not hard to picture in the reeds the hulks of eighteenth century ships which used to come to Glaslyn Bridge before Porthmadog and the Embankment were built.

The Nantmor

Difficulty: Grade IVe
Access: Gelli-Lago (G.R.632483)
Egress: Bwlchgwernog (G.R.611452)
Distance: 4 kilometres
Portages: One or two forced by fences and trees across the river

Introduction

If you can bring yourself to take seriously a ten foot wide stream that has the same grade as the Grand Canyon of the Colorado River, then this river is a must. It is Welsh hill canoeing par excellence; low bridges, even lower trees, and two tiny gorges with continuous Grade IV water.

The Nantmor rises in the Moelwyns, a group of hills neither particularly high nor extensive, but much used by local outdoor centres for teaching and assessing mountain navigation. I have a theory that the foot-trenches which have developed on the popular routes as a result of this use, have increased the drainage of the Moelwyns out of all proportion to its area. Perhaps that is why the Nantmor is canoeable after *very* heavy rain?

Similar in character to the Nantygwryd, it is yet more continuous, but without any big falls, and more atmospheric, although it has none of the views. Care is needed throughout, as a tree could easily block the river, and there is wire across in three places.

The River

Between Llyn Gwynant and Llyn Dinas, four kilometres north-east of Beddgelert, a small road branches off to the south-east. Follow this road through two gates and round a sharp right-angled bend, until, after four kilometres, at Gelli-Lago, that mighty torrent, which is the Nantmor, starts to become visible! Access is best made at a bridge over the stream - an old quarry on the other side of the road is the most obvious landmark.

Launch if you dare, but be sure to face downstream as there is no room to turn a canoe for some hundred metres. A bridge, carrying the road across to the left bank, soon appears and then an easy section before the first gorge. Just below the first drop into the gorge, and dangerously out of sight round a corner, there is a fence across the river. This will almost certainly have to be *portaged*. The rest of the gorge is exciting and very tight (IVd).

A short interlude leads to the second, and more serious gorge (IVe).

Near the top the stream divides, a sharp left turn necessary to take the very narrow left shoot. Someone on the bank is a sensible precaution against getting jammed here. The water is Grade IV for another half kilometre, and then widens and flattens.

The remainder of the Nantmor is technically Grade II and III, but remains serious (d) because of the close overhanging branches, fallen trees, and two barbed wire fences (it is possible to go under these). This last tree lined section is about two kilometres in length. Half way down a large house, Dolfriog (G.R.614458), is prominent on the right bank. A rope course is strung across the river here.

Egress from the river is best made at Bwlchgwernog, where a road crosses the river - the second bridge over it (this road joins the Nantmor road one hundred metres to the east). It is possible to continue down to another bridge (carrying the A.4085), or indeed into the lower reaches of the Glaslyn, but white water enthusiasts will not be so interested in these stretches.

So there it is, The Mighty Midget of the Moelwyns. Wait until the other rivers are chocolate brown, and you cannot fail to have an amusing and exciting time on this little stream; an experience not to be missed.

The Colwyn

Difficulty: Grade IVe (One fall of Ve)
Access: Hafod Ruffydd Isaf (G.R.575498)
Egress: Warws (G.R.587482)
Length: 3 kilometres

Introduction
The Colwyn is a very exciting, albeit short, pool-drop river, with some serious paddling needing close inspection. The A.4085 Caernarvon to Beddgelert road, south of Rhyd-Ddu, runs parallel to the river, access, although not inspection, being easy to and from it. The Colwyn drains the south-western slopes of Snowdon, and the eastern side of the Nantle Ridge, and is best paddled from below the junction of the tributaries flowing out of these two watersheds. It flows into the Glaslyn at Beddgelert, and therefore can be combined with the Aberglaslyn Gorge to form one of the best wild water trips in North Wales.

The River

A forest track (metalled) leads west off the A.4085 to Hafod Ruffydd Isaf, close to the confluence of the Colwyn's two main tributaries. Driving from Beddgelert this is the first left turn after the Forestry Commission Campsite (G.R.578490). Put in just below the bridge over the eastern tributary.

A kilometre of tight technical paddling over bedrock steps leads to the Forestry Commission Campsite (on the right) and an exciting rapid under the bridge (IVd). Two or three hundred metres below this bridge, there is a two-tier fall called *'Paddle Test'*, which is preceded by a nasty little drop with a submerged boulder blocking the main channel. Paddle Test at IVe is serious but not highly technical, except in high water when it becomes Ve. This series of rapids needs close inspection and probably bank security. The plunge pools below have been well 'tested'.

The river now continues through some excellent rapids, including a notable one with a powerful diagonal stopper, into Beddgelert. The third road bridge appears (G.R.585482), and below it the meanest rapid of them all, *'Dragon's Tail'* (Ve). The bridge, and rapid, are just above Warws, a prominent shop on the road out of Beddgelert. A good view of this hard rapid may be had from the bridge, and looking upstream a depth gauge is visible. A good level for Dragon's Tail, and for the rest of the river, seems to be around 4.

The Colwyn becomes progressively easier below Dragon's Tail, until it has become flat where it joins the Glaslyn. It is perhaps best therefore, to get out below the last rapids - behind the carpark at Warws, - unless you intend continuing down the Aberglaslyn Gorge. In that case you will be well juiced with adrenalin, no rehearsal necessary for the water ahead.

*Canogging on the frozen Lynnau Mymbyr,
below Snowdon.   Photo: Derek Mayes*

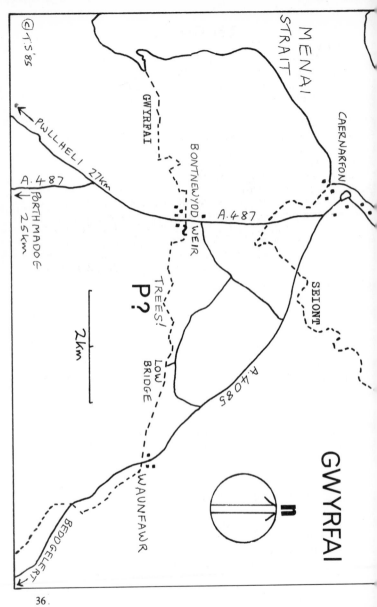

GWYRFAI

MENAI STRAIT

© T.S'85

PWLLHELI 27km

A.487

PORTHMADOG 25km

GWYRFAI

BONTNEWYDD WEIR

A.487

CAERNARFON

SEIONT

A.4085

P?

TREES!

LOW BRIDGE

2km

WAUNFAWR

BEDDGELERT

n

The Gwyrfai

Difficulty: Grade IIId
Access: Waunfawr Bridge (G.R.525590)
Egress: Bontnewydd Bridge (G.R.482598)
Portages: Several short carries may be necessary
Length: 5 kilometres

Introduction

Aquatic dinosaurs (long necks and no brains) will enjoy the Gwyrfai. Never has the twin grading system been more useful - Grade III for the water, and Grade d for the trees. So it is only possible to recommend the river to donits (done it all) or gofers (go for it) who are looking for more excitement. In spate, it is dangerous, because the river flows through woods on either side, and even in average flood, there will be branches and trees across the river, forcing the occasional portage. Still, rather like the Mirkwood of Tolkien's imagination, which the surrounding tangle of trees resembles, this river seems to hold a morbid fascination for local canoeists. There is no reason, therefore, why others would not find the trip equally 'interesting'.

The River

The Caernarvon to Beddgelert road (A.4085) passes over the Gwyrfai at Betws Garmon and Waunfawr. Between Betws Garmon and Waunfawr the river is too small to canoe, so a small lay-by at Waunfawr bridge is the best access point. The river is immediately technical, Grade IIIc, and remains so until the small bridge below Plas Glanrafon (G.R.508595). This bridge will decapitate, so it must be portaged; it has also on occasions proved a useful escape route back to the main road.

From Glanyrafon to Bontnewydd, the Gwyrfai digs deeper into the valley and flows with greater power. There are no very big falls on the river, but this section is Grade IIId due to the potential obstructions and lack of break-outs. Some portages will be necessary, depending on the damage done by the winter storms. There is also a weir near Bontnewydd which most will want to portage. It is possible to put in again and canoe to the sea. After Bontnewydd, however, the river loses all technical interest, so the bridge in this village is the best egress point.

The Gwyrfai is a short trip - hardly five kilometres - but it is one packed with interest. The technical interest indeed is so continuous that the canoeist will find it impossible to remember sections in any detail. So, should you want to canoe the Gwyrfai again, it will continue to hold out plenty of surprises!

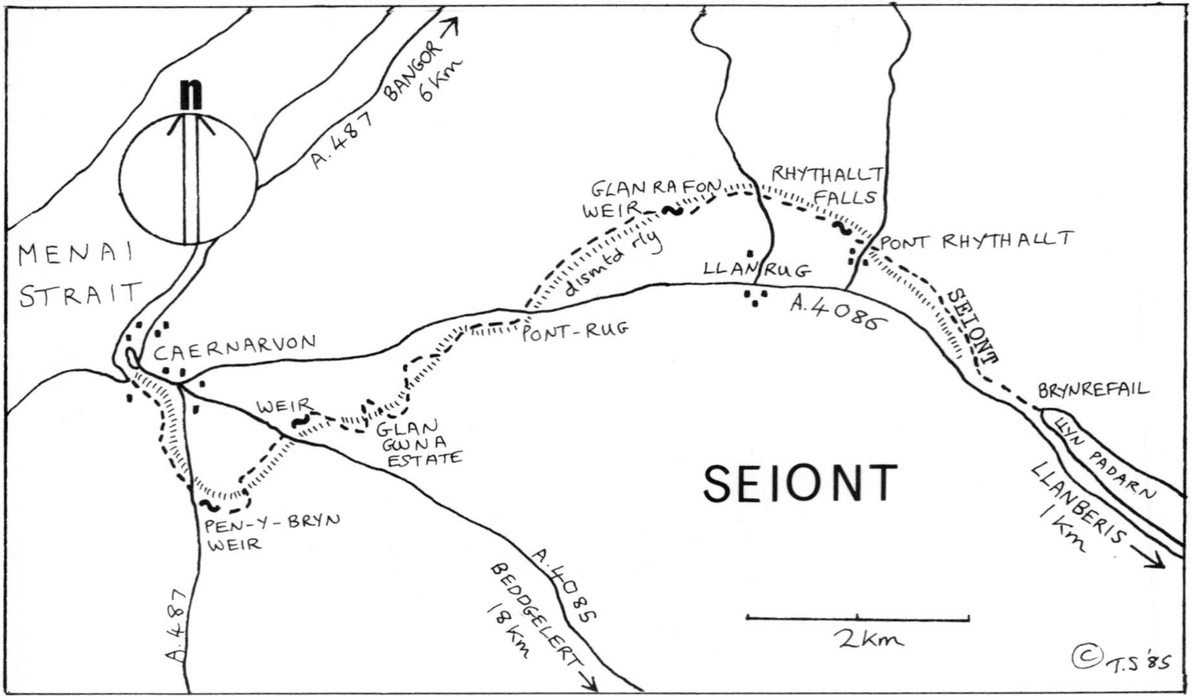
n
MENAI STRAIT
A.487
BANGOR 6 Km
CAERNARVON
WEIR
GLAN GWNA ESTATE
PEN-Y-BRYN WEIR
A.487
A.4085
BEDDGELERT 18 Km
PONT-RUG
dismtd rly
GLAN RAFON WEIR
RHYTHALLT FALLS
LLANRUG
PONT RHYTHALLT
A.4086
SEIONT
BRYNREFAIL
LLYN PADARN
LLANBERIS 1 Km
SEIONT
2Km
© T.S '85

The Seiont

Difficulty: Grade IIIc (one fall of IVc)
Access: Pont-Rhythallt (G.R.543636)
Egress: Caernarfon Castle (G.R.476626)
Length: 11 kilometres

Introduction

The Afon Seiont is not a beautiful river. Flowing from slate tips, beside factories, and into a town of 15,000 people, it has less of the mountain mystique and wooded charm typical of other Welsh rivers. For all that, it is an aesthetic trip for the canoeist. Over 9 kilometres between lake and shore and no portages, it is a river which brings you without landfall to the tide; like a mountain climb which emerges on the summit without artificial aid, this has an appeal all of its own. And the canoeing is good; eleven kilometres of fairly continuous grade IIIc through rapids and weirs, which particularly in high water, require skill and judgement.

The River

The purist will want to start the Seiont at its source, Llyn Padarn. This lake, however, having almost recovered from the ravages of Dinorwic, the largest slate quarry in the world, has now lost one million cubic feet of its shore to the Central Electricity Board's pump storage scheme. An equally good start for the canoeist therefore, is Pont-Rhythallt two kilometres downstream; for unless you like slate tips and turbine tunnels, you will only be missing a stretch of flat water.

Rhythallt Falls (IVc), the hardest on the river, comes half a kilometre after Pont-Rhythallt. It may be inspected from either bank, but a good view can be had from the course of the old railway line which runs parallel to the Seiont for the whole of its length - close on the right bank at this point. There follows a kilometre of water broken by small weirs. Under a road bridge and then into the Bryn Afon steps, a series of small natural drops through gorse and bracken country, exciting even when the river is low. A sharp right hand bend leads through a dismantled bridge on the old railway line, and then the river widens as it approaches Glanrafon farm (G.R.522641).

It is worth inspecting the weir below this farm, and the island which follows, for it was on just such a stretch of the Seiont, where the branches hang low, that a near fatal canoeing accident occured. In high water the penalties for a poor line of descent on this river are out of all proportion to the technical difficulty of the canoeing.

Next comes probably the best of the river; 2 kilometres of grade IIIc with a sharp left-hand bend and the Caernarfon-Llanberis road bridge (G.R.512631) marking the middle of this section. After this, the river twists and turns each way, seemingly trying to avoid the houses and factories which crowd its edge. One bridge you will remember if the river is high, for after turning a log blocking the left hand channel, you must duck to avoid its girders.

The largest weir on the river catches you unawares, on a flat section half a kilometre after the Glan Gwna housing estate (G.R.493622). Possibly, for this reason, the back-tow in the stopper feels strong. That done, there is only the broken weir at Pen-y-bryn to shoot, and you are in salt water. This back entrance to Caernarfon harbour is surely the most striking finish to any river trip in North Wales. One moment you are kayak king on a little river, the next a dwarf boat drifting amongst the rotting clippers and paint-bright catamarans. And where else could you draw your canoe out under the shadow of a 13th century castle, its towers guarding the western end of the Menai Straits?

The Ogwen

Difficulty: Sections of IIId, IVc, and IVd (Ve in flood).
Access: Ogwen Bank (G.R.624656); Scout Hut Bridge
(G.R.610677).
Egress: A.5. Bridge (G.R.607689); A.55 Bridge (G.R.602708);
River Mouth (G.R.613720).
Length: 9 kilometres

Introduction

There is no doubt about it, the Ogwen is one good river. It is
continuously hard, but nowhere desperate, and, without portages to
interrupt the flow, provides a really satisfying paddle from the
mountains to the sea.

The Ogwen is fed by the northern Carneddau and Glyders, and, like
many of the rivers of Snowdonia, rises and falls quickly. The best
place to judge the water level is at Scout Hut Bridge. If all the
boulders are covered the river is in full flood, and a serious proposition
at Grade Ve. Normally many boulders are clear, and it is then a steady
IVd.

The hardest sections of the river are through gorges, so that, in
flood, the flow is concentrated rather than dispersed. However, the
gorges are shallow and open enough to allow easy inspection, more
like Scottish glens than true gorges.

BETHESDA GORGE - OGWEN BANK TO
SCOUT HUT BRIDGE

Grade IVc; 3 Kilometres

Ogwen Bank Caravan Park lies just south of the town of Bethesda,
close between the A.5. and the Ogwen. *Ogwen Bank Falls* is a spike
strewn weir which as J.H. wrote 'is best ignored by all except suicidal
scrap metal merchants'. Needless to say it has now been canoed.

There follows the *Gun Barrel*, an exciting shoot of water channelled
by the quarrymen in the last century. The Gun Barrel ends in a steep
rapid containing some sharp boulders. Those wishing to miss this
section can put in at the next bridge (G.R.626659), which carries the
B.4366 over the river. To reach this bridge turn first left on entering
Bethesda from the south.

Easy water now leads to the start of Bethesda Gorge. The start of the
difficulties is marked by a sharp right-hand bend - known as *Bethesda
Falls*, it is most awkward in low water. A footbridge follows and a
couple of steep drops, which are washed out in very high water. The

41

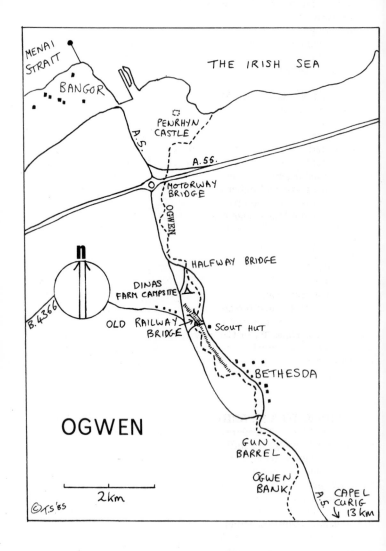

canoeing is not serious, but can be tricky with waves rebounding off the bedrock walls.

On leaving Bethesda the river flattens out, and the open banks and fields sometimes provide a lucky sanctuary for unaccompanied canoes. There is then nothing of interest until the lead-in to Fishermans' Gorge.

FISHERMENS' GORGE - SCOUT HUT BRIDGE TO A.5. BRIDGE
Grade IVd; 2 Kilometres

A broken weir three hundred metres above Scout Hut Bridge (named after the Hertfordshire Scouts' building which is next to the bridge on the right bank) heralds the start of this classic section. A steep rapid with holes and big waves follows, with, in high water, two big stoppers forming just above and under the bridge. An eddy on the right just below the bridge is a good place to take stock.

Between Scout Hut Bridge and the A.5. Bridge there are two tree covered islands. The first, immediately below the railway viaduct, is taken on the right. The second, beside Dinas Farm Campsite (G.R.609685), is fairly obviously shot on the left. About half way between these islands there is a large fall on the left ending in a nasty stopper. Below Dinas Farm Campsite the difficulties become less continuously technical.

The whole of the superb section of water as far as the second island can be inspected from a tiny path on the right bank. The difficult section beside Dinas Farm Campsite is best checked from the left bank, after an awkward eddy-out just above. In high water prior inspection is recommended since eddies are hard to find. As a whole this stretch of the Ogwen ranks amongst the best wild water in Great Britain.

A.5. BRIDGE TO A.55. BRIDGE (OR RIVER MOUTH)
Grade IIId; 3 (or 4) Kilometres

Below the A.5. Bridge the difficulties ease somewhat, but there is still continuous white water almost as far as the sea. High up trees can be a problem, and lower down there are a number of broken weirs which need watching in flood conditions.

The North Wales expressway now crosses the lower Ogwen, it's foundations forming a new rapid. The next bridge below this concrete giant is a more traditional structure carrying the A.55. A council depot is just upstream on the left. This is the easiest place to get out, although the purist, who wants to finish on salt water, can drive his vehicle to the very mouth of the river. Those choosing this second option will, on a clear day, see Puffin Island appear round the last bend in the river, a suitably calming antithesis to the excitement above.

Fighting a haystack, on the Tryweryn Slalom Course.
Photo: Ken Fidler

Cobdens Falls, on the Llugwy well off the flood.
Photo: Terry Storry

45

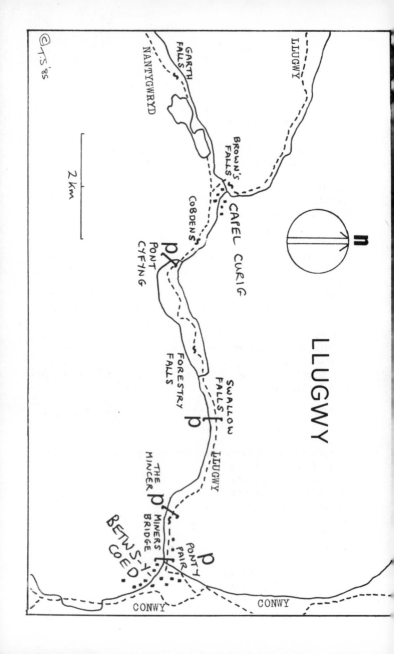

The Llugwy

Difficulty: Sections of Grade IIIc, IIId, IVc (with falls of IVd and Ve).
Access: Ogwen Valley (G.R.698596); Plas y Brenin (G.R.716577); Pont Cyfyng - below (G.R.735569); Ugly House (G.R.756574).
Egress: Browns Falls (G.R.720571); Pont Cyfyng - above (G.R.733571); Ugly House (G.R. as above); Pont y Pair (G.R.790566).
Portages: Pont Cyfyng (G.R.734572); Swallow Falls (G.R.765577); The Mincer (G.R.779570).
Length: 14 Kilometres

Introduction

The Llugwy is probably the most popular touring river in North Wales. This is (traditionally) because of the lack of access problems; it is also partly due to the proximity of outdoor centres (notably Plas y Brenin and The Towers); above all however, it is because the Llugwy is a friendly river for the average canoeist. Certainly this is the primary reason for the steady use, for more than twenty years now, of the stretch between Plas y Brenin and the Ugly House. However, there are also difficult and dangerous rapids on this river, some recently canoed, made feasible by plastic boats, but three remaining as portages, where something more than superb skill and good equipment are needed.

THE UPPER LLUGWY - EFFLUENT OF NANT Y GORS TO CONFLUENCE WITH NANTYGWYRD

Grade IVc (one fall of Ve); 4 Kilometres
From Fynnon Llugwy reservoir the Llugwy rushes into the Ogwen valley to be joined by other streams as it heads towards the small village of Capel Curig. During and shortly after *heavy* rain it can be paddled from the junction with one of these streams - the Nant y Gors - coming out of Galt y Ogof. Below this junction the Llugwy comes conveniently close to the neighbouring A.5. and access can be made anywhere along this road.

Flat at first, the Llugwy soon becomes strewn with boulders, technical but not serious (IIIb). A stand of pines is passed on the left after one kilometre, and the canoeing becomes more difficult over bedrock steps (IVc). A girder in the middle of the river marks the lead in to *Brown's Falls* (Ve), one hundred metres below. Those wishing to portage this commiting and difficult drop can get out above the girder to the road on the left, or, more carefully, just above Brown's Falls, to the field on the right.

Brown's Falls lies behind 'Joe Brown's' climbing shop in Capel Curig, and can be readily inspected from the bridge just below. The most obvious line lies down the right-hand side beneath low branches. In high water a big stopper lurks beneath the bridge. There remains only a succession of standing waves and a sharp left hand bend, before the Llugwy goes under the A.4087 and joins the Nantygwyrd.

THE MIDDLE LLUGWY - PLAS Y BRENIN
TO UGLY HOUSE

Grade IIIc (one fall of IVd); 6 kilometres; one portage

Plas y Brenin, the National Centre for Mountain Activities, is in fact on the Nantygwyrd, a sporting little river described elsewhere in this Guide. It is however, the logical put-in for this classic section of the Llugwy. A public footpath leads down to Pont y Bala, the footbridge below P.Y.B. at the eastern end of the twin lakes, from a gate beside the former hotel.

There is a pleasant little manufactured chute below Pont y Bala, and then flat water as far as the confluence with the Llugwy. The combined river now flows strongly over little rapids until *Jims Bridge* appears behind an island. The rapid here is an excellent training ground for novices (IIb). As an indication of the incredible fluctuations in the Llugwy's water level, it is worth noting that, once or twice a year, the concrete ramp connecting the forestry bridge to the main road (A.5.) forms a small stopper on it's downstream side.

Below Jims Bridge the rapid peters out and flat water heralds the run in to *Cobdens* (IVd). To inspect this rapid and the little drop - *The Slot* (IIIc) - which precedes it, it is best to get out on the right bank to a forestry track and path, which leads to the bridge below Cobdens, a good place for photography and other spectator sports. The Slot catches many unawares, and prompt action is required to prevent an unoccupied boat from proceeding over Cobdens. It is possible to get out below the Slot to the road on the left by some steps over the otherwise vertical wall. Cobdens itself is best shot over the central slab, which should be well covered. The water tends to carry you right, down a mean little gully, but that route is only advisable in high water to avoid stoppers in the middle. In very high water, when no rocks are visible, Cobdens can be Grade Ve. Should the water be at that level a stiff drink in the neighbouring hotel of the same name may serve to harden the resolve, or mollify the spirit.

Jim's Bridge on the Llugwy.   Photo: Derek Mayes

A sharp right-hand bend below Cobdens leads to a pleasant little rapid by another watering hole - the Tyn y Coed Hotel. If you have come to grief above, and you prefer to drown yourself, rather than your sorrows, then you can continue over Pont Cyfyng Falls five hundred metres below. All but the last corkscrew drop has now been canoed (in low water), but few will want to emulate this feat, or be the first down the final chicane. Fortunately there is flat water above the waterfall and bridge, and egress is simple to fields on either bank. Do however, get out in good time.

Below the portage at Pont Cyfyng access is from the right bank down a muddy path beside the Worsley Wardley O.P.C. Cottage. From here down to the A.5. roadbridge (Ugly House), the rapids are frequent, but never hard. Notable is *The Graveyard* (IIIb), a long rapid next to the sewerage works, after five hundred metres, and *Forestry Falls* (IIIc), dividing round an island at the top and forming a classic tongue through a stopper at the bottom, after three kilometres. Forestry is an excellent finale to this stretch of river. It is possible to egress on the left just below the A.5. roadbridge to Ugly House carpark, or, alternatively, some three hundred metres upstream to a small road which follows the right bank of the Llugwy from Pont Cyfyng.

Cobdens Falls, on the Llugwy, in low water.   Photo: Terry Storry

THE LOWER LLUGWY - UGLY HOUSE TO PONT Y PAIR

Grade IIId (one fall of IVd); 4 kilometres; two portages

On reaching Ugly House many will want to get out, but for the adventurous an isolated and exciting section of the Llugwy remains. Despite the portage at Swallow Falls this is the best place to start. Approach the top of Swallow Falls with great caution, and get out before the last rapids on the left bank. Five years ago Hargreaves wrote that, 'any proposed attempts on this waterfall should be negotiated with the Swallow Falls Hotel opposite, who control the turnstile used by paying tourists visiting this beauty spot; you should be able to double the entrance fee at least! Those lacking a sense of humour, please be warned, Swallow Falls is definitely a portage'. Now however, rumours abound that even *The Swallow* has been done - by the main drop, in very low water.

A difficult portage takes you down the left bank of the river to below Swallow Falls; a rope may be found useful for lowering canoes. Put in above a short rapid (IIIc) on a right-hand bend, and continue for a kilometre through boulder fields and over small drops. The river is wide so any fallen trees from the surrounding forest are easily avoided, but a good flood is needed to fill this conduit for canoeing. At the bottom of this superb ravine, there is a narrowing of the river ending in a notable stopper, surprisingly mean even in low water (IIId). Egress should be made just after this on the right bank by some wooden seats, in order to avoid *The Mincer*, a very nasty double drop with a boulder blocking the only feasible route. The Mincer has been canoed, but constitutes a very serious problem (VIf).

A path winds round The Mincer on the right bank, leading to steps down to *Miners Bridge* (G.R.780569). Here is an exciting rapid possible at quite low levels. By carrying up the right bank a little way it is possible to put into the pool just below The Mincer. The narrow channel under the bridge is committing and unpredictable (IVd).

Below Miners Bridge, and for about one kilometre, the Llugwy remains technical and intricate (IIIc). Fortunately it eases considerably before cascading over Pont y Pair Falls (another noted tourist attraction of Betws y Coed), thus allowing the wary, or weary paddler to reach the car park on the left, before taking the plunge.

Pont y Pair Falls (Vf) was first canoed some fifteen years ago, but has seen few, if any, repeats; this is hardly surprising, since it needs a rare flood to submerge the massive central rock. When this is covered a line over the top seems feasible, but the paddler must then contend with a nasty stopper beneath the bridge. In the conditions necessary to make the main fall possible, this is not a good place to practice rolling. Below there is nothing of interest until the Llugwy joins the Conwy for a more sedate journey to the sea.

Forestry Falls, on the Llugwy, in flood.   Photo: Stewart Brooks

The Nantygwryd

Difficulty: Grade IVc (one fall of IVd)
Access: Pen-y-Gwryd (G.R.663559)
Egress: Plas-y-Brenin (G.R.716577)
Portage: Llys Falls (G.R.669559)
Length: 6 Kilometres

Introduction

Like the very top section of the Llugwy, the Nantygwryd is a small stream which drops rapidly after rainfall. It really needs to be raining at the time to paddle it. That said, it is an exciting and enjoyable paddle, with a steep gorge at the top, and a good fall at the bottom. Views of the surrounding mountains are unrestricted, and can be enjoyed at leisure on the finishing paddle across the twin lakes.

The River

Access is by a bridge carrying the A.4086 over the stream just below the Pen-y-Gwryd Hotel. An exciting kilometre of Grade IVc leads down to *Llys Falls* (Vf), a small waterfall one hundred metres below the Nant-y-Llys, the first major stream entering from the right. Further warning of its approach is given by a fallen concrete stanchion, and then the remains of an iron bridge just above the fall itself. Most will want to *portage* this fall and everyone to inspect it, egress being effected by driving the boat on to the grassy banks.

Below Llys Falls, the Nantygwryd is Grade IIIb and IIb as far as *Garth Farm Falls (IVd)*, a big drop easily seen from the road and needing much water to blot out some large boulders in the centre. A route down the right hand side is easier than it looks, and a bridge just above the falls gives plenty of warning.

After Garth Farm Falls the river flows into the twin lakes, Llynnau Mymbyr, and out again by a small rapid under Pont-y-Bala the bridge at Plas y Brenin. This is a good practice rapid for novices, and egress is possible on either bank. It is now possible, of course, to continue down the Llugwy, which the Nantygwryd joins half a kilometre below.

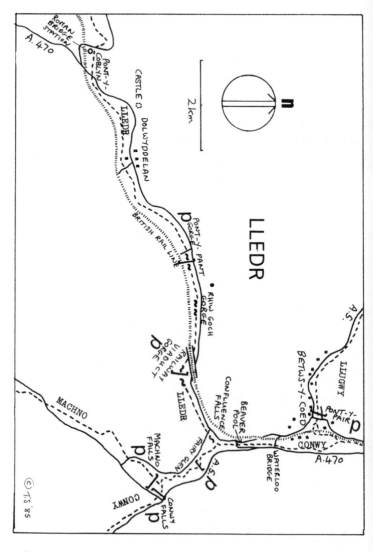

The Lledr

Difficulty: Sections of Grade IIIc, IVc, and Ve
Access: Roman Bridge (G.R.710515); Pont-y-Pant
(G.R.758538)
Egress: Pont-y-Pant (G.R.755538); Beaver Pool (G.R.798547)
Portages: Pont-y-Pant Gorge (G.R.756538); Viaduct Gorge
(G.R.780537)
Length: 9 kilometres

Introduction
The Lledr is perhaps too easy and hard by extremes to become famous among canoeists. Nevertheless it contains two of the great challenges of North Wales, and long sections of Grade III in a very beautiful valley. Those not keen to make a name for themselves in the gorges, will find the portages relatively easy, while still leaving plenty enough of excitement in the river. In short the Lledr is a welcome addition to the guide.

ROMAN BRIDGE STATION TO PONT-Y-PANT
Grade IVc; 5 kilometres
The technical interest on this section lies right at the beginning, where the river is very narrow and drops steeply over boulders. Not long after Pont-y-Coblyn the river flattens out and becomes quite placid through Dolwyddelan. Access to this stretch is from a small road turning right off the A.470 just after Pont-y-Coblyn.

PONT-Y-PANT TO CONFLUENCE WITH CONWY
Grade Ve; 4 kilometres; two portages
This section contains three short gorges, only the middle of which has been paddled. Between the gorges there is easier, but still interesting canoeing. To avoid the top gorge at Pont-y-Pant, put in just below, on either bank. The other two gorges are easily carried on the right bank. So this stretch is an enjoyable paddle at Grade IIIc.

Pont-y-Pant Gorge is one of the great challenges of North Wales (Vf). There is certainly a line down it, but a capsize here would be unthinkable. The last drop eases to Grade IVd, and then below there is a kilometre of Grade IIIc. A double fall (IVc) warns of the beginning of the second gorge, at Rhiw Goch, just below.

Rhiw Goch Gorge (Ve) is easier than Pont-y-Pant, but the last drop contains a very nasty boulder right in the middle. This, and the three falls above, which constitute the gorge, are not highly technical, but are serious and very exciting, particularly in high water. The rapids are, in order of descent, *Twist and Turn, Rock, Roll, and Rooster Tail.*

Below Rhiw Goch Gorge the Lledr is Grade IIIb as far as the railway viaduct. The river divides round an island just before the viaduct, giving an interesting drop (IIIc) and warning of things to come. *Viaduct Gorge* is the hardest section of the Lledr (Grade VIf). It might just be possible at low water, but it has yet to be attempted. The main problem is the narrowness of the gorge forcing tight turns in very turbulent water. A successful descent would be more by luck than judgement. Egress above the gorge is easily made just beside the viaduct, and a simple portage down the right bank leads to easier water below.

Below Viaduct Gorge the river is again IIIb, and continuously interesting at that Grade for a kilometre. Finally four technical drops (IIIc) close together precede the confluence with the Conwy. *Bridge Falls* consists of two drops, one before and one just after, a tiny road bridge. The third, called *Pencil Sharpener*, corkscrews through a four foot wide slot, and the last, *Drop Off,* has a good line on the left and a nasty hole on the right.

Finish down the Conwy for a few hundred yards and get out below the A.470 road bridge in Beaver Pool. The rapid here (IIIb) will seem tame after the excitement above. Next time the gorges?

The Upper Gorge of the Conwy.
Photo: Terry Storry

The Conwy

Difficulty: Sections of Grade IIb, IIIc, IVc, and Ve
Access and Egress: Pennant Farm (G.R.824469); Junction
Merddwr/Conwy (G.R.855511); Roadbridge (G.R.827524);
Above Conwy Falls (G.R.812533); Below Conwy Falls
(G.R.808534 & G.R.805537); Beaver Pool (G.R.798547);
Waterloo Bridge (G.R.798558)
Portages: Pandy Uchaf (G.R.839484); Conwy Falls
(G.R.809533); in Fairy Glen (G.R.802538)
Distance: 14 kilometres

Introduction
With few equals among the rivers of Snowdonia is the Afon Conwy.
Con*way* it was to the English, who guarded its entrance with their
most powerful Welsh castle. Broad, flat, and English it is too, in its
lower half, where the flood plain provides rich farm land and two golf
courses. But just twenty kilometres from its mouth, above Betws-y-
Coed, where the river flows beside the London to Holyhead road
(A.5), the Conwy shows its true descent from the hills.

There is Beaver Pool and the Fairy Glen, an innocuous name for the
two kilometres of turmoil which begins with the Conwy Falls.
Nothing English in that, nor in the somewhat easier ten or eleven
kilometres of the Upper Conwy twisting and turning in the contours
above. White where it falls, green as it eddies, this is a canoeist's world
in a series of gorges isolated from the world above.

PENNANT FARM TO CONFLUENCE WITH MERDDWR
Grade IIIc (One fall of IVc); 5 kilometres; one portage
After heavy rain it is possible to canoe from below Pennant Farm to
the junction with the Afon Merddwr. This section is grade IIIc,
except for a fall at Ysbyty Ifan (G.R.842486) which is IVc. Between
Pennant and Ysbyty there is a dangerous fall to be portaged below
Pandy Uchaf. This is fairly obvious as you approach, and is best
carried on the right bank.

Ysbyty Falls may be inspected from either bank, and is best canoed
from left to right. Warning of the falls is given by a steep, but not
dangerous weir, just above. The only other time you may want to leave
your canoe, is to look at *Hargreaves Folly*, a grade IIIc slot below
Bryniau Defaid Farm (G.R.855503).

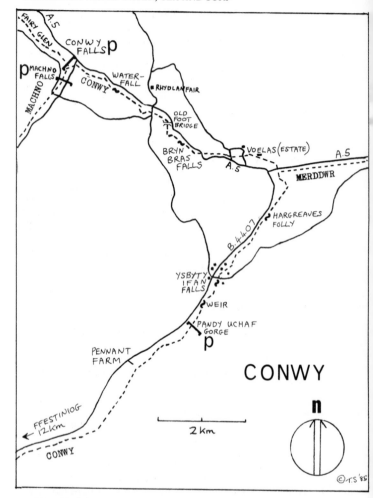

THE UPPER GORGE - CONFLUENCE WITH MERDDWR TO RHYDLANFAIR BRIDGE

Grade IIIc (One fall of IVc); 4 kilometres

Light and technical so far, the Conwy passes under Telford's A.5 and picks up the Afon Merddwr, becoming stronger. The river digs deep with this new power and for the next 2 kilometres steep rock and grass rise 50 to 100 metres on each bank. Half a kilometre of grade IIc in the new water before a footbridge and then a road bridge into the Voelas estate mark the start of continuous grade IIIc. Another 300 metres in the gorge and there is a second road bridge high above. Find an eddy hereabouts to savour the river, for this is the very best of it; a steep rock and water world, where neither walker nor swimmer may go in comfort.

The next rapid you will perhaps remember. A sharp left hand bend hiding a rock the size of a barn, and then the Padog Farm narrows, 200 metres in length, 10 metres in width. A pause for breath, and then off again, under the A.5 road bridge to meet the Afon Eidda cascading in from the left. Still grade IIIc here, and the falls below Bryn Bras Farm in sight. You may have inspected the Bryn Bras falls from the A.5 as it runs parallel, but the way is fairly obvious. First right, then left, then right again to avoid the submerged rocks ahead, and finally through the stopper at the bottom (IVc). Now the river relaxes, and after a kilometre you will pass under a rickety footbridge. This marks the end of the rapids on this section, and a further half kilometre below, the bridge taking the road to Rhydlanfair appears round a corner, egress on the left bank. This is a good point to finish, if Grade III is what you came for, because the river now drops more steeply as it heads towards the Conwy Falls.

THE LOWER GORGE - RHYDLANFAIR BRIDGE TO CONWY FALLS
Grade IVc (One fall of Ve); 2 kilometres
For those who have only now warmed to the sport, there remains two kilometres of river, easy at first, becoming, in the end, continuous grade IVc. Like the Upper Gorge, this section of the Conwy has the merit of being canoeable (in plastic boats) at low water levels. However there is a Grade Ve waterfall half-way down this stretch, which has recently been canoed, but which most will want to portage, particularly in high water. Below, there is good canoeing, but care should be taken to egress one hundred metres above the road bridge on the left bank. Looking over the Penmachno road bridge into the Conwy Falls, you may thank the river for that little waterfall of a warning.

THE FAIRY GLEN - CONWY FALLS TO BEAVER POOL
Grade Ve; 2 kilometres; one portage
The Conwy Falls should be avoided (although it has recently had its

first descent,) but below the last waterfall, the *Fairy Glen* offers one of the best sections of wild water in Wales. The best access for this hairy stretch of water is from a small road between the Penmachno Woollen Mill (G.R.806528) and the A.470 (turn south at a small stone bridge over the bottom of the Lledr). The road runs down the left bank of the river, and from the top lay-by one must scramble through a wood and down a steep bank to get to the water. A fallen tree poses problems on one of the early drops, and then, after a narrow gorge section, there is a Grade VIf rapid, which, to date, has **not** been canoed - portage on right bank. The second section of narrow gorge should not be missed -access down the steep bank below the portage. Below the last big fall, which unnervingly is impossible to inspect from the river, the Fairy Glen eases to Grade IIIc for the last half kilometre. A footpath comes down the right bank, at this point, from a track leading up the east side of Beaver Pool. This is a popular access point for tourists, and useful for anyone wanting to paddle the easier lower section of the Glen. The Fairy Glen may be paddled at very low water, but is probably best in medium spate; in high water it is Grade VIf.

The confluence with the Lledr lies below the last drop in the Fairy Glen, and a short steep fall (IIIc) at the bottom of that river can easily be added to your trip. Otherwise the rapid (IIIb) just above Beaver Pool will bounce the paddler happily towards his vehicle. Access and egress at Beaver Pool is by a lay-by on the left bank just below the bridge.

BEAVER POOL TO WATERLOO BRIDGE
Grade IIb; 1 kilometre
The Conwy now relaxes as it spreads out towards the sea. There is still however, a short section of white water as far as Waterloo Bridge in Betws-y-Coed. In high water this section is excellent value at the grade, one which novices will enjoy. Egress at Waterloo Bridge is on the left bank opposite the filling station.

A Fragile Environment
The Conwy has, and will, get a lot of traffic. It is a great canoeing river. It is also a community of plants and animals who have to live there when the canoeist has gone home. From Pennant Farm down to the Conwy Falls the river hosts a number of endangered species, including the otter. It is an area of special concern to conservationists. In order to preserve this fragile environment, canoeists are asked not to *'play'* on the Conwy. A straight run on this river will in any case be the natural choice for most canoeists. It will effectively reduce our in-

trusion into the shaky ecology of the area. As always our motto should be 'take only pictures, leave only footprints'.

'Simply messing about in boats' - the weir above Irish Bridge on the Tryweryn.   Photo: Derek Mayes

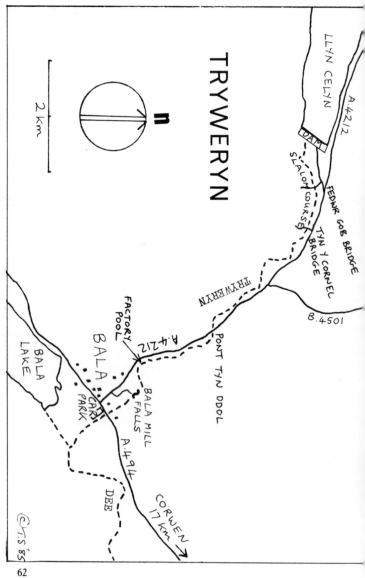

The Tryweryn

Difficulty: Sections of Grade IIIb and IVc; but see note at the end on variations in water release.
Access: Llyn Celyn Dam (G.R.881398); Tyn y Cornel Bridge (G.R.895399); Factory Pool (G.R.920367)
Egress: Tyn y Cornel Bridge (G.R. as above); Factory Pool (G.R. as above); Pont Tryweryn (G.R.929362)
Length: 8 kilometres

Introduction

The story of the fisherman in his waders being swamped by the rising waters of the Tryweryn is probably apocryphal. The experience of canoeists being left high and dry by fast falling water is not. For the Tryweryn is a dam controlled river, changing from trickle to flood, babble to roar (and back again), in a matter of minutes. The canoeist therefore, needs to pick up the phone, rather than look out of the window, when deciding whether to go on the Tryweryn. And if the tap has been turned on, he can be sure of company on this river; for having been the site of the 1981 World Championships, it is internationally famous.

At first glance, the Tryweryn will do nothing to diminish the apprehension inspired by its international status. Seemingly happy to be released from the unnatural confines of Llyn Celyn, the water swirls past the fish traps, and surges on down the upper section of the river in a series of apparently non-stop rapids. On closer aquaintance however, the Tryweryn feels friendly enough, and even the continuous top section is not hard by international standards. Lower down, the Tryweryn is even more gentle, and excepting Bala Mill Falls, may be paddled by the novice white water canoeist. On the upper slalom course, the water is more channelled than usual in the Welsh hills, but not dangerously so. In short, whatever your standard, the Tryweryn is good value.

LLYN CELYN DAM TO TYN Y CORNEL BRIDGE

Grade IVc; 2 kilometres

Access is below the fish pass under the dam, reached from the picturesque A.4212 lakeside road by a turn-off at Ciltalgarth, five kilometres north-west of Bala (G.R.892401). The first series of drops appear after a left hand bend, three hundred metres downstream from the dam. This marks the start of *The Graveyard*, a boulder field of a hundred metres. Below are a couple of channelled stoppers and then

Fedwrgog Falls on the Tryweryn. Photo: Terry Storry

the start of the *Upper Slalom Course.* A particular fall to look out for, early on in the Course, is the Fedwrgog falls, which is just below the first bridge over the river (G.R.889401). This fall, and the difficult lead-in above, is easily seen and inspected from the road up to the dam. The left hand arch of the bridge is blocked by boulders, and a large diagonal stopper sits below the right hand arch. This fall is most easily shot close to the right bank.

Two hundred metres further downstream, a sharp right angled bend leads you into a large eddy on the right bank. Standing waves and a shoot with angled stoppers on either side follow, and then a double fall with a notable haystack wave. Finally, in this section, there is a steep weir, its approach marked by a large boulder on the left, supporting a cushion of water. The easiest line passes close to the boulder to take the weir on the right. And so to the bottom of the upper slalom course. Many will want to exit on the right to a field before Tyn y Cornel Bridge (camping allowed here), carry their boats up the bank, and put in again just above Fedwr Falls. This is the best of the Tryweryn, and for some the only part they will paddle.

Bala Mill Falls on the Tryweryn.   Photo: Terry Storry

TYN Y CORNEL BRIDGE TO FACTORY POOL
Grade IIIb; 5 kilometres
Below the top section, the river broadens and flattens into 5 kilometres of Grade IIIb technical and scenic in its own way. It would be a shame to miss this more gentle interlude, particularly since there are some very interesting little rapids. Egress in Factory Pool is by way of a footpath to the road (A.4212), which is close on the right bank at this point.

FACTORY POOL TO PONT TRYWERYN
Grade IVc; 1 kilometre
Access is by a footpath on the right bank of the river. A series of rapids leads to *Bala Mill Falls* (IVc) after eight hundred metres. Although this lower slalom site is much shorter than the first, it is also harder in the straight run. It is easily inspected from the right bank, where a tree overhangs and rocks jut into the river. A chicken shoot on the left is much used by white water racers, but those in slalom boats can shoot the main fall on the right without too much problem. A good place for photographs this, since it is possible to walk in from the road. A car park on the right bank, just below Pont Tryweryn (the A.494 road bridge), is the best place to get out.

THE NATIONAL WHITE WATER CENTRE

The Tryweryn is an exceptional Welsh river in two ways. Access to it is part owned by the British Canoe Union. It is therefore paddled by more people than any other. Indeed, so much is it being used that the flow of the river has been artificially concentrated, and dangerous boulders removed in order to further improve it for canoeing. Secondly, the rise and fall of the river is determined by human, rather than meteorological, agents. Changes in water level can therefore, be predicted, and paddling plans made in advance.

All other things being equal, there are eleven days each year when a release of water is guaranteed, and these are reserved for competitive canoeing events. In addition there are about one hundred and eighty days when a release, of some kind, is made for operational purposes, and the river is available for canoeing. Access to the water from the Dam to Tyn y Cornel Bridge is all the year round; access to the lower part of the river is only guaranteed outside the fishing season. The fishing season lasts from March to October.

Access to the Tryweryn is the responsibility of the Canoeing Management Officer, and, when the Dam is releasing, he can usually be found at The National White Water Centre beside the upper slalom site. An 'ansaphone' is in operation to advise on water levels and availability. The number is Bala (0678) 520826. The following levels will be used on the ansaphone.

Very Low: Unsuitable for canoeing
Low: Only limited use possible; plastic boats advised; Grade IIb
One third volume: Plastic boats advised; Grade IIIb
Two third volume: Grade IIIc
Full volume: Grade IVc; 250 million gallons a day

The term 'release' may be used on the phone, instead of 'volume'.

The Dee

Difficulty: Sections of IIb, IIIb, and IVd
Access: Carrog Bridge (G.R.114437); Horseshoe Falls - below
(G.R.195432); Llangollen (G.R.216420); Trevor Rocks (G.R.267420)
Egress: Horseshoe Falls - above (G.R.194433); Llangollen (G.R. as
above); Newbridge (G.R.287417)
Length: 23 kilometres

Introduction
The Afon Dyfrdwy, or as the Saxons called it the River Dee, is the
best known of all the North Welsh rivers. For long it has been a
popular touring river, canoeable even after a drought from Bala
(confluence with the Tryweryn) to Connahs Quay, a distance of
eighty-two miles. More recently three stretches of the Dee, in the Vale
of Llangollen, have become popular with white water enthusiasts; the
first running from Carrog past Glyndyfrdwy to Horseshoe Falls, the
second from Horseshoe Falls to Llangollen Town, and the third from
Llangollen to Newbridge.

'The best stretch of the Dee is that from Glyndyfrdwy to Horseshoe
Falls', said the B.C.U. Guide to British Waterways (1961). 'From
there to Llangollen is generally regarded as being too difficult and is
best avoided by transferring to the canal'. This was out of date even as
it was written. The trip from Horseshoe Falls to Llangollen is not only
one to which any competent canoeist can aspire, but is by most
standards the best on the river. The principal rapids of the Serpents
Tail and the Town Falls are venues for major slalom competitions, and
the whole stretch provides an excellent white water racing course. Big
waves, stoppers, and exciting drops, all contribute to make this, in
medium to high water, the classic white water run.

Nevertheless, the upper valley of the Dee, which in Welsh is called
Glyn-dyfrdwy - that is the valley of the Dwy or Dee - is certainly the
most beautiful part of the river; and with a number of small rapids, it
is not without interest. Moreover, this part of the river, falling over
more even ground, changes less in character with variations in water
level, than the steeper sections below.

Only slightly harder than this upper section, is the lower stretch
from Llangollen to Newbridge. It is less scenic than the upper vale,
but has a good rapid at Trevor and a number of other worthwhile
stretches of water. For novices in white water canoeing it is well worth
considering.

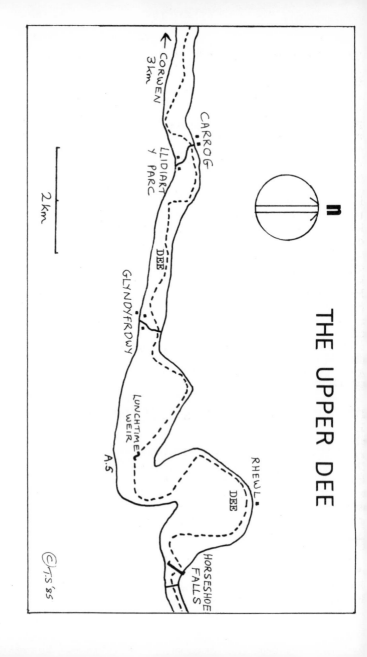

THE UPPER DEE

N

2 km

← CORWEN 3 km

CARROG

LLIDIART Y PARC

DEE

GLYNDYFRDWY

LUNCHTIME WEIR

A.5

RHEWL

DEE

HORSESHOE FALLS

© T.S '85

THE UPPER DEE - CARROG BRIDGE TO HORSESHOE FALLS

Grade IIb; 11 kilometres

Access above Carrog Bridge on the right bank is straight-forward, it being reached from the A.5 by turning north at Llidiart y parc. A small rapid under the bridge is a good place to warm up, and a measure of things to come. From here to Glyndyfrdwy (alternative access point on the right bank below the bridge - G.R. 150430) is three and a half kilometres and small rapids are interspersed with flatter sections.

Below the high and narrow bridge at Glyndyfrdwy somewhat more interesting rapids appear. One drop called *Lunchtime Weir*, because of the convenient seats just below on the left, has an excellent wave in low water, but is washed out in high water. Other longer rapids lower down the river are better in flood conditions.

After eight kilometres the road on the left bank runs beside the river offering a convenient get-out to a lay-by. Better however to continue and so include the excellent Berwyn Rapids (IIb), finishing the trip at Horseshoe Falls. This dangerous weir is not all that obvious round a right hand bend, although unnaturally slack water above and a dull roar below will give some clue. Egress is above the weir on the left bank.

The really energetic may extend this trip a further five kilometres at the same standard by putting in above Carrog, at Corwen where the A.5 crosses the river. Access is from a track below the bridge on the left bank.

THE LOWER DEE - HORSESHOE FALLS TO LLANGOLLEN

Grade IVd; 3 kilometres

The last few years have seen the advent of mass tours on the Dee, organised by the Mike Jones Memorial Fund and Manchester Canoe Club, and in the classic section from Horseshoe Falls to Llangollen this has led to a new absurdity in canoeing practice - the eddy queue and a new technique - the raft for support. Well known and much used this section may be, but it can still spring the odd and sometimes unpleasant surprise. The Town Falls demands respect, the Serpents Tail is not easily mastered, and the weirs in between are harder than they look.

Horseshoe Falls acts as the feeder for the Shropshire Union Canal which follows the left bank of the river. When full the canal offers a pleasant return trip for the 'unshuttled' driver. Access below Horseshoe Falls is on the left bank by taking the steep metal staircase

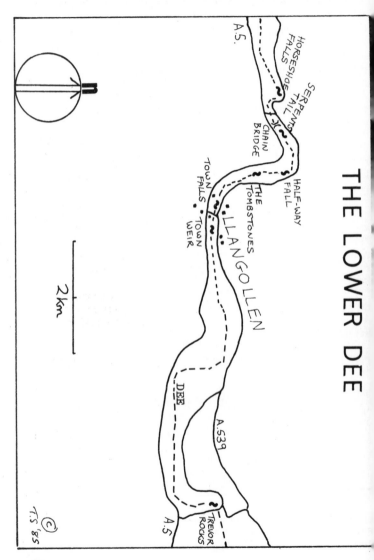

THE LOWER DEE

down from Chain Bridge Hotel carpark over the canal to the tow path and following this upstream for two hundred metres. *Horseshoe Falls* can be shot on the left fairly safely by a broken double drop (IIIc), but the main weir is very dangerous (IIIe).

Easy water leads down to the Chain Bridge with a good rapid just above (IIIc). Below the bridge the main flow leads down right to the Serpents Tail after five hundred metres, while in high water a succession of stoppers forms over rocks and sills on the left. One look at the *Serpents Tail* (IVc) - from a convenient rock shelf on the left, only flooded out in very high water - will convince many of the deep breathing technique - 'take a deep breath youth and go for it'. At low water there is a pronounced drop at the top, while in flood a big stopper forms at the bottom, and in between the waves always seem big, the eddies vicious. However this is a safe place to swim as many *'gofers'*, cardboard canoeists, and inner tubists have found. And for the expert it is a good place to play.

After the final sharp meanders of the Tail a flat section leads to a broken weir (IIIc). This is best shot on the left where a sharp eddy cut allows good upstream crosses - beware of iron spikes in low water. Another smaller rapid precedes the railway bridge, and then there is *Half Way Weir* shot either on the left or, in high water by a thin tongue in the middle. Half Way Weir with its long diagonal stopper is easily seen from the back road to Llangollen (IIIc).

Next comes another broken weir with two concrete stanchions visible in the centre - the 'Tombstones'. *Tombstones* (IIId) has been responsible for one drowning and several near misses with paddlers wrapped broadside around the stanchions. The weir is usually shot on the extreme left although routes down the middle and right are quite exciting particularly in high water.

Shortly after Tombstones there is a perfect play stopper where the following excuses for not rolling may be found useful - 'I was sucked out of my boat', 'my spraydeck was ripped off', and 'my paddle was torn out of my hand'. Most of us, of course, have developed a comprehensive list of such lies to suit each occasion. Without prompt action from a rescuer the 'ripped', 'torn', and 'sucked' may swim over the next rapid, the last before Town Falls. *Factory Weir* (IIIc) is to the left of an island (the factory, now disused, is on the right), the main channel forming standing waves, and in high water a superb hole, on the left-hand bend.

The lead-in to *Town Falls* follows, and those wishing to inspect the rapid should get out beside a wall on the right bank when the bridge comes into view. It is both difficult to choose, and to find, the perfect line down *Town Falls* (IVd). It is a long and complicated rapid with three distinct drops. The first is a weir easily taken in the middle by a little spout. The second called *The Pot* can be shot anywhere, but most easily right of middle. The Pot leads right to the falls proper which are just above the bridge and to the right of an island. A route close to the island or the right bank seems preferable, but you may have little choice in the matter. In high water it is possible to go to the left of the island through big waves and stoppers.

One hundred metres below the bridge is *Town Weir*, broken and easily shot on the left (IIIc), but forming a very nasty canoe gobbling stopper on the right (IVf). Prompt action below the bridge is required by friends and strangers to catch the damp and dispossessed from Town Falls. Organisers of events have been sufficiently concerned about this weir to post rescuers above, and divers below, and I know from personal experience that prevention is easier to effect than the cure. Egress is on the left bank just below the weir; a concrete path leads back to the road.

THE LOWER DEE - LLANGOLLEN TO NEWBRIDGE
Grade IIIb; 9 kilometres

The five kilometres between Llangollen and Trevor Rocks (first bridge after Llangollen) is sometimes used for white water races when the river is in high flood, but it is of no great interest to white water addicts. However, the next four kilometres are certainly worthwhile, starting at Trevor Rocks, finishing at Newbridge.

Access to *Trevor Rocks* is from the north side of the river (left bank) by a minor road upstream of the bridge. This rapid (IIIb) was the site of the first slalom competition held in Britain (1939), and remains a good training rapid. Between Trevor Rocks and Newbridge the rapids are easier but quite entertaining for the novice. The river passes under the canal (half a kilometre), the railway (three kilometres), and then the road, this 'new' bridge marking the egress point. To reach the A.483 it is best to scramble up the right bank.

Langdon Bank Buoy on the crossing of Holyhead Bay.
Photomontage: Derek Mayes

THE
SEA GUIDE

Sea Canoeing and the Guide

This Guide seeks to attract and stimulate canoeists, to be read by the fireside as well as on the beach. I have used a personal style, and included much non-essential, but nonetheless interesting, information. All the key facts are here - tide races and tidal streams, overfalls, buoyage and lights, access and egress, distances, and prominent features - but it is not an objective listing. For those wanting such an approach there is always the Admiralty Pilot, and the Admiralty Chart.

Forecasts

The Sea Canoeist needs to do some homework before embarking on any of the trips described. The Guide will help, but it cannot replace good planning and good judgement. The most important factor to be borne in mind is the weather. Here, nothing is certain, except that it will change; and changes in the weather, particularly in wind speed and direction, can dramatically alter the nature of the trips. A shipping forecast for the relevant Sea Area, - *Irish Sea* - can be obtained, day or night, from Holyhead Coastguard (Tel: 0407 2051). They will also give information on local wind speeds and sea states. They have worked extensively with local sea canoeists, and are friendly and sympathetic to our sport.

Rescue

The coastguard can be more than a source of information. In 1984, Holyhead Sub-Station, which is responsible for the area from the Dee Estuary to Barmouth, had 284 call-outs. None of these involved experienced sea canoeists, but should an accident happen, rescue may depend on the Coastguard knowing your plans - destination, time of arrival and departure, number in party, colour of canoe, and whether you are carrying flares. And let them know when you arrive safely.

Descriptions

The sea trip descriptions in this Guide are in clockwise order round the coast of North Wales - as are the descriptions of Surf beaches, and Coastguard and Lifeboat Stations (see Appendix III). A map follows each description, except in the case of Rhoscolyn, Penrhyn Mawr, and The Stacks, all of which are represented on the map of Holy Island. The descriptions (and maps) are selective, and canoeists may want to consult other sources for further information (see Appendix VI).

When reading the descriptions, the following points should be borne in mind. Winds are described by the direction *from* which they blow, but tidal streams are described by the direction *to* which they flow. Whenever applicable, compass points, and left and right, relate to direction of travel (trips are described in one direction only, that direction implying *no* preference, unless stated). A phrase such as 'passed *to* the right or west' means that the object is on the canoeist's right or west, while a phrase such as 'passed *on* the right or west' means that the object is on the canoeist's left or east.

Grid references are given in the descriptions, but when they are in the notes at the beginning, they are not repeated in the text. Grid references are taken from the appropriate 1:50,000 map of the area, six figure references being accurate to 100 metres, and four figure references to 1 kilometre. These references are to be preferred for accuracy to the marked features on the Guide Book maps. Wherever distances are given, they are accurate only to the nearest kilometre. Occasionally miles are used, and this is always nautical miles, again accurate to the nearest whole number.

Maps

The Guide Book maps are not substitutes for the Admiralty Charts, and the latter should be referred to whenever possible (see Appendix VI). The maps are sketches, with important information highlighted and confusing detail eliminated. Under the principle that a picture is worth a thousand words, they will give the reader a quick overall guide to the trips.

A number of signs, symbols, and abbreviations, have been used on the sea maps. These are listed below. It is important to note that the strength of the tidal streams is *not* indicated by the number of feathers on the arrows (except in the case of the two Tidal Stream Maps), but

〰〰	Tide Race and/or Overfalls	L.W.(S).	Low Water (Slack) - also used in descriptions.
←1-3	Direction of Ebb Stream		
＼＼＼→	Direction of Flood Stream	M.	Nautical Miles
B.W.	Beacon	Mo.	Morse
B.Y.	Buoy	Occ.	Occulting
C.G.	Coastguard	Occas.	Occasionally
Ev.	Every	R.	Red
Fl.	Flashing	Rk.	Rock
H.W.(S)	High Water (Slack) - also used in descriptions.	Sec.	Seconds
		T.	Tower
L.B.	Lifeboat	Vis.	Visibility
L.H.	Lighthouse	Wr.	Wreck
L.S.	Landing Stage		

rather by the numbers above the arrows. The lower number indicates the average rate on neaps, the higher number gives the average rate on springs.

Access

The high tide mark is the upper limit of Crown Property. Below that level there should be no problems of access or egress. Above it however, only a public right of way secures untroubled put-ins and landings. Wherever possible I have suggested access and egress where such a right of way exists, but sometimes there is no such right, and in any case, such agreements change from time to time. So, mention of access or egress in the Guide is no evidence of the right to launch or land. Whenever in doubt, ask the local landowner for permission.

Apart from local people along the coast, the canoeist must consider another population which lives on the edge of the sea. Sea birds, between early February and late July, make the cliffs of North Wales their home. They are easily disturbed by canoeists on land and on the sea. Local paddlers are observing a voluntary ban on landing near nesting sites in this period, and try to keep a hundred metres offshore wherever there is nesting activity. Auks (Guillemots, Razorbills and Puffins) are most easily disturbed, and one of their favourite sites is the cliffs opposite South Stack. Climbers do not go here in spring and early summer, and if you are paddling through South Stack Gully in this period, please pass as quietly as the water.

Tides and Tidal Streams

North Wales is host to big tides and strong tidal streams. Plans for most of the trips in this Guide will need to take them into account. Specifically the canoeist will need to know three things; the direction of the tidal stream (ebb and flood), the times this stream changes direction (Slack Water), and the strength of the stream (rate). If the latter is 1 knot or less, he can forget about tidal streams. But a quick look at the Flood and Ebb Stream Maps which follow, will show that round North Wales this is not common.

The Ebb and Flood

Off North Wales the flood goes north up the Irish Sea, while the ebb goes south (the north going flood stream reaches a latitude of 54 degrees north, just south of the Isle of Man). Close in, the streams generally run parallel with the coast. The precise direction of the ebb and flood, and the eddies caused by these streams, is much dependent on the particular configuration of the coastline. Details of the inshore streams are on the guide book maps and in the written descriptions.

Slack Water

The stream changes direction about once every six hours, although, as always, there are exceptions - for example the Inland Sea. Off North Wales, the ebb is stronger than the flood and tends to run for longer. The ebb usually runs for considerably more than six hours, while the flood usually runs for slightly less than six hours. The combined effect of this is to advance the time of Slack Water High and Slack Water Low by about three quarters of an hour every twenty-four hours.

The stream is said to be Slack at that instant when its direction of travel is reversed (for practical purposes the stream is usually slack for about half an hour). Slack Water does not always coincide with the time of High and Low Water. For instance, at Menai Bridge Slack Water occurs an hour and a half before High and Low Water. To find out in which direction the stream is going therefore, the canoeist needs to know the time of Slack Water, rather than the time of High and Low Water.

The time of Slack Water (and High and Low Water) varies, on any day, up and down the coastline. In North Wales, the further north you are, the later, in general, will be the time of Slack Water. The tidal stream off the Lleyn Peninsula for instance, changes direction between one and two hours before the stream off Anglesey. The *Slack Water Constant* is the time by which Slack Water, at ports round the

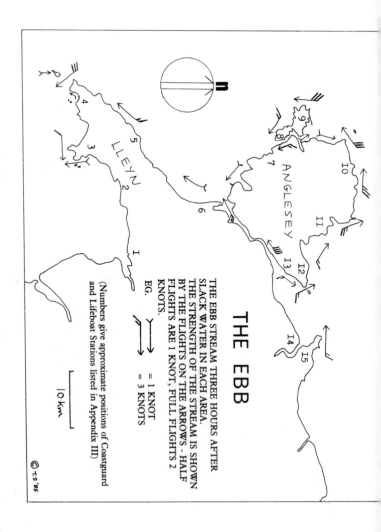

THE EBB

THE EBB STREAM THREE HOURS AFTER
SLACK WATER IN EACH AREA.
THE STRENGTH OF THE STREAM IS SHOWN
BY THE FLIGHTS ON THE ARROWS - HALF
FLIGHTS ARE 1 KNOT, FULL FLIGHTS 2
KNOTS.

EG.
⟶ = 1 KNOT
⟶ = 3 KNOTS

(Numbers give approximate positions of Coastguard
and Lifeboat Stations listed in Appendix III)

10 km

© T.S. '86

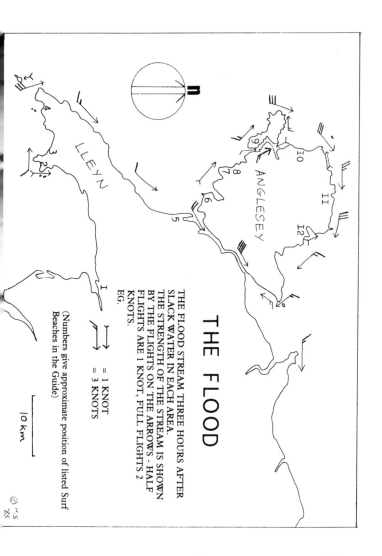

THE FLOOD

THE FLOOD STREAM THREE HOURS AFTER
SLACK WATER IN EACH AREA.
THE STRENGTH OF THE STREAM IS SHOWN
BY THE FLIGHTS ON THE ARROWS - HALF
FLIGHTS ARE 1 KNOT, FULL FLIGHTS 2
KNOTS.
EG.

= 1 KNOT
= 3 KNOTS

(Numbers give approximate position of listed Surf
Beaches in the Guide)

10 km

LLEYN

ANGLESEY

© T.S '85

coast, varies from High and Low Water at *Liverpool.* A Slack Water Constant is given for each trip described in the Guide.

To work out the time of Slack Water at a particular place, add, or more usually subtract, the Slack Water Constant from the time of High and Low Water at Liverpool on the day in question. Liverpool Tide Tables are readily available from local shops all round the coast, and are very cheap. The times in the tables are based on Greenwich Mean Time, so between March 31st and October 27th, an extra hour should be added to any computations, to take account of British Summer Time.

The table below summarises the information (given in the Guide) on Slack Water Constants, and also shows the High and Low Water Constants for the area. It is thus possible to see at a glance where the time of Slack Water differs from the time of High and Low Water. To my knowledge this information has never before been collated in a systematic way. This is not surprising really, because shipping and yachting are more interested in the vertical movement of the local tides (to find out drying heights and channel depths), than in the precise horizontal movement of the inshore tidal streams.

Tidal Stream Rates

The direction of the tidal stream, and the time it changes direction, are not the only concerns of the sea canoeist. The strength of the tidal stream is also very important. Anglesey and the Lleyn have some of the strongest tidal streams in the country, always pleasing to paddle with, sometimes impossible to paddle against, and occasionally frightening in their effects.

The rate or strength of the tidal stream changes hourly, daily, and monthly. The hourly change occurs over *about* six hours, which is the interval between successive Slack Waters (with a few exceptions - see, for instance, Penrhyn Mawr). To calculate the rate of tidal streams at any one time, and this formula differs slightly from that in the Almanacs, use the 'Thirds' rule - 1/3, 2/3, 3/3, 3/3, 2/3, 1/3 of maximum rate at the time. The maximum rates for spring and neap tides are given in the description and shown on the maps in this Guide. Except in a few important cases, which are mentioned in the Guide, the stream is at the maximum rate around half time between the changes of direction, and at a minimum at the time of Slack Water. The duration of Slack Water - when the stream is ¼ knot or less - varies from place to place along the coast and is longer on neaps than on springs - an average is given for each trip.

TIDAL CONSTANTS

Average Tidal Differences, which when applied to High(H) and Low(L) Water(W) at Liverpool, will give the approximate time of Slack(S) Water, High Water and Low Water, at the place in question (G.M.T.)

Place	Slack Water Constant	High/ Low Water Constant
Tudwals	-3.20	-3.20
Bardsey	Mainland Inshore -3.00 Offshore -1.50 Bardsey Island -1.00	− 3.30
Lleyn, North Coast	-2.15	-2.00
Llandwyn Island	-1.50	-1.50
Rhoscolyn	Penrhos Bay & Offshore -1.30 Rhoscolyn Sound -3.00	1.15
Penrhyn Mawr	H.W.S. -1.15 L.W.S. -2.30	1.10
South Stack	-1.10	-1.10
North Stack	H.W.S. -2.00 L.W.S. -1.00	-1.00
Holyhead	H.W.S.-2.00 L.W.S. -1.00	-0.48
Inland Sea	H.W.S. +1.00 L.W.S. +2.00	H.W. +1.00 L.W. +2.00
Carmel Head	H.W.S. -1.15 L.W.S. -2.15	-1.50
Skerries	-1.15	-0.50
Anglesey, North Coast	Coastal -0.45 Offshore -1.15	-0.45
Anglesey, East Coast	-0.30	-0.45
Dulas Bay North Shore	H.W.S. -3.30 L.W.S. -0.30	-0.45
Puffin Island	H.W.S. +0.30 L.W.S. -0.40	-0.45
Menai Bridge	-2.00	-0.30
Caernarfon	-1.15	-1.35
Ormes	-0.25	-0.25
Chester	H.W.S. +1.05	H.W. +1.05
Connah's Quay	No info.	H.W. +0.25
Sharpness	No info.	H.W. +4.54

The strength of the tidal stream changes daily, because the gravitational pull of the moon varies according to its position in the heavens. Spring tides occur a little after both New and Full Moons, in other words fortnightly. Neap tides also occur fortnightly, halfway between each Spring tide, a little after the First and Last Quarters of the moon. *Tide height and range is greater on Springs, as is the rate of tidal streams.*

The height of the tides on each day of the year is shown in the Liverpool Tide Tables, so it is easy to see when the tide is on the 'Make' (increasing up to Springs); when the tide is 'Taking Off' (decreasing towards neaps); and when the streams are at their weakest and strongest. As an indication, a High Water height of more than 9 metres at Liverpool indicates fairly powerful (Spring) streams around the North Wales Coast, while a High Water height of less than 8 metres indicates fairly weak (Neap) streams.

About twice a year the High Water height at Liverpool goes above 10 metres, and half way between these two times, the Spring height barely goes above 9 metres. This monthly cycle, caused by the changing relationship of the sun to the moon, and both to earth, produces extra strong Spring tidal streams near the Vernal (21st March) and Autumnal (23rd September) Equinoxes. Weak Spring tidal streams will be found in January and July.

Finally, it should be noted that Slack Water times, and tidal stream rates, are affected by local winds, approaching depressions, and low barometric pressures. In particular, off the North Wales coast, strong winds between south and west, and depressions approaching the coast rapidly from the west, are likely to increase the strength of the flood stream, and decrease the rate of the ebb stream. Low barometric pressures, by raising the sea level, may increase the rate of both flood and ebb. These variations caused by the weather, serve as a useful reminder of a general rule, namely that *the Slack Water Constants, and tidal stream rates, given in this Guide, are approximations.*

The Tudwals

Access: Marchros (G.R.318264)
Egress: Porth Ceiriad (G.R.12284); or Hells Mouth (G.R.286260)
Distance: 6 kilometres or 13 kilometres
Max Rate of Tidal Streams: 3 knots (springs), 1½ knots (neaps)
Tide Races and Overfalls: None
Slack Water Constant: -3.20
Duration of Slack Water: 0.30 to 1.00

Introduction

In the smoking rooms of the Royal Yacht Squadron, the names Tudwal East and Tudwal West are probably not on everyone's lips. Nevertheless, for the sea canoeist visiting or living in North Wales, the Tudwals offer an uncomplicated paddle in interesting coastal scenery. It can be combined with a couple of hours surfing in Port Ceiriad or Hell's Mouth, making a really good day's outing.

The Islands

St. Tudwal's Islands consist of two small islands lying off the eastern flank of Penrhyn Du, the nearest to the mainland being the West Island, that further offshore, the East Island. Northward of the Islands is a black conical buoy called 'Sandspit', and, from Abersoch on the ebb, a course past 'Sandspit' will take you nicely on to the East Island. From Marchros is shorter, but it is necessary, if going on the ebb, to aim off slightly to the north of East Island to make landfall there.

From a naturalist's point of view, Tudwal East is the more interesting of the two Islands. There is a large population of seabirds here, including kittiwakes and fulmars. The best landing place is halfway down the eastern side of the Island. There is no shelter, apart from a small ruin at the southern end.

The West Island is similarly barren, except for the automatic lighthouse (Fl WR ev 20 sec, Vis 13M), and its attendant buildings, where newspapers from the 1950's and old sofas are home for a band of fleas. Landing is easiest at some steps at the north-eastern extremity of the Island. Apart from the deserted lighthouse, there is a good bivouac site about one hundred metres north of the southern tip of the Island on the west side. This is only accessible from the sea, and is somewhat open to winds from the south-west.

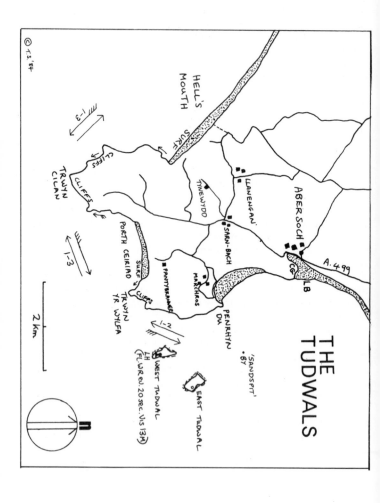

Tidal Streams

The tidal streams in St.Tudwals Sound and round the islands are not strong, never more than 2 knots on springs. So it would be possible, if more arduous, to visit at unfavourable states of the tide. The favourable streams are the ebb from Abersoch or Marchros, and the flood from Hell's Mouth or Porth Ceiriad.

However, navigating the headlands of Trwyn Yr Wylfa, and more especially Trwyn Cilan, against the prevailing stream (particularly the stronger ebb which runs at up to 3 knots) will pose problems on springs. One way would be to sneak through very close to the cliffs, but this is not to be recommended in rough weather. So, if you are intending to paddle round the headlands, some tidal planning is advisable.

THE HEADLANDS

Trwyn Yr Wylfa is a small headland dividing St.Tudwal Sound from Porth Ceiriad and is swiftly rounded. Porth Ceiriad is an attractive little beach backed by high cliffs. A way down to it may be found through Pantybranner farmhouse and fields, with parking and a campsite above the beach (payment at the farmhouse). This is a good surf beach in a southerly swell, with the best waves being found in the south-east corner of the bay. There can be surf here, when it is flat at Hell's Mouth.

Trwyn Cilan is a much bigger headland, dividing Porth Ceiriad from Hell's Mouth to the west. For three kilometres the headland is ringed by continuous steep cliffs offering no possibility of landing, an awe inspiring place. Once into Hell's Mouth there is likely to be surf if the prevailing winds (south-westerlies) have been blowing. It is certainly the best known of the North Wales surf beaches, and there will be 'boardies' here when the 'greenies' are running. Again the best breaks are to be found in the south-east corner of the beach, and access to this is by way of Tynewydd, and then along the muddy tracks and fields. Camping is possible here by arrangement with the farm. Alternatively, there is public access from the road south of Llanengan. But, on summer weekends, be prepared to be boxed in by Pink Floyd vibrating V.W. camper vans propped up by blonde gods waxing their planks.

Bardsey

Access: Aberdaron (G.R.170263)
Egress: Porth Oer (G.R.165298)
Distance: 18 kilometres
Max. Rate of Tidal Streams: 6 knots (springs), 3 knots (neaps).
Overfalls and Tide Races: Carreg Ddu, Braich y Pwll, Maen Bugail, Bardsey Sound.
Slack Water Constant: Mainland Inshore -3.00; Offshore, including Bardsey Sound - 1.50; Bardsey Island Inshore -1.00; (Note: H.W. and L.W. is -3.30).
Duration of Slack: 1.00 (Mainland Inshore); 0.15 to 0.30 (Offshore incl. Bardsey Sound *and* Bardsey Island)

Introduction

Bardsey is a serious offshore paddle through big water, involving detailed tidal planning. Tidal calculations are particularly difficult here, because of the different times of slack water around Bardsey, and because the paddler must cross, rather than go with, the stream. And the stream is very strong; Bardsey Sound is a mean place to be in rough weather.

Having said that, the Nature Reserve of Bardsey Island is one of the most relaxing and beautiful in Britain. The three squat kilometres of grassy hillside are grazed by sheep and the occasional horse, while the old farmhouse buildings are now rented to bird watchers, who make the longer crossing from Pwllheli every Saturday from May to September. Unlike many of the skerries dotted around Anglesey and the Lleyn, this feels like a place to stop; to sunbathe amongst the lobster pots perhaps, or swap stories by a driftwood fire at dusk, as the manx shearwaters assemble offshore in their dense rafts.

ABERDARON BAY

Aberdaron Bay is a friendly little seaside town with a number of good pubs. Access to the sand and shingle beach is by way of a slipway leading from the centre of the town. The beach, which is about a mile long, forms the northern shore of Aberdaron Bay. In south or south-westerly winds there is often surf here. It has a tendency to dump, and there are rocks to look out for close to the beach.

The western side of the bay is formed by a range of cliffs, partly carved away, no doubt, by the strong eddy stream which, on the ebb, runs south south-west along this shore. On the east side of the bay and continuing the axis of the headland - Trwyn Gwningaer - are two

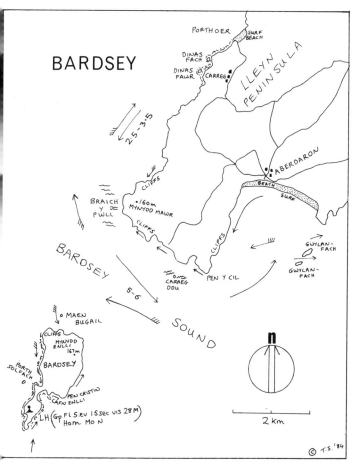

BARDSEY

PORTH OER — SURF BEACH

DINAS FACH

DINAS FAWR — CARREG

LLEYN PENINSULA

2·5 - 3·5

CLIFFS

BRAICH Y PWLL

•160m MYNYDD MAWR

ABERDARON

BEACH SURF

CLIFFS

CLIFFS

BARDSEY

5 - 6

SOUND

•CARREG DDU

PEN Y CIL

GWYLAN-FACH

GWYLAN-FACH

o MAEN BUGAIL

CLIFFS

MYNYDD ENLLI 167m

BARDSEY

PORTH SOLFACH

PEN CRISTIN CAFN ENLLI

LH (Gp Fl 5.ev 15sec vis 28M) Horn Mo N

n

2 km

© T.S. '84

islands, Ynys Gwylan-fawr and Ynys Gwylan-bach. These are sometimes called 'Seagull Islands' although cormorants and puffins are the most common breeding birds. Seals also seem to like the place, and there is an interesting selection of plants. Landing is quite easy in calm weather. The ebb stream runs quite strongly between the islands, and also between the islands and the headland, in a southerly direction.

87

BARDSEY SOUND

Approaching Bardsey Sound from Aberdaron it is perhaps best to leave with the last of the ebb, while the strong eddy stream formed in the lee of Pen y Cil is still running south-west. This will enable the paddler to reach Pen y Cil quickly, and then to cross Bardsey Sound on the first of the flood. Half way across Bardsey Sound, the last of the ebb will still be running south-east, which will help correct the north-westerly drift of the young flood close inshore to both the mainland and Bardsey.

The other realistic alternative for the canoeist crossing to Bardsey from Aberdaron, is to use the last of the flood, or the start of the ebb, to reach Pen-y-Cil, and then ferry glide across Bardsey Sound using the north-eastern corner of the island as a heading.

On the trip suggested in this guide, it is best to return to Braich y Pwll on the flood, and use the same tide up the north-west coast of the Lleyn. Some however, may wish to return to Aberdaron, in which case the ebb is the easiest phase of the tide to use. The narrow eddy stream - about fifty yards across -which runs north up the eastern side of Bardsey on the ebb, allows the canoeist to reach the northern tip of the island, whence a ferry glide against the ebb brings him back into Aberdaron Bay. Here, of course, it is best to keep out from the west shore, to avoid the eddy current.

The Admiralty Pilot warns, 'vessels without local knowledge not to use Bardsey Sound except with a favourable tide'. This is also good advice for the canoeist, who will find it impossible to make headway against the strength of the stream in the Sound. However, it is possible to *cross* the Sound at any state of the tide (not weather), by making use of the enormous eddies which form at either end of the Island. These eddies extend for an incredible two kilometres, a north-going eddy off the southern tip of Bardsey on the ebb, and a south-going eddy off the northern tip of the Island on the flood. Thus having missed Bardsey by bad judgement, poor timing, or lack of sessions in the multi-gym, the paddler can go for the biggest break-out in North Wales, and use it to make landfall. Needless to say, this can be a more lengthy, not to say worrying, way to cross Bardsey Sound.

The Sound has a number of overfalls. That off Carreg Ddu, an above water rock some two hundred metres off the headland near Pen y Cil, is best known to canoeists, for it is almost continuous on both flood and ebb, and has strong return eddies, making it an excellent place for 'playing'. There is also a tide race and overfalls off Braich y Pwll, and around Maen Bugail, the latter chiefly on the ebb. On both states of the tide, a small shoal half a kilometre to the west of Bardsey lighthouse causes overfalls. All these areas of rough water are obvious in calm weather, but when the wind is blowing, particularly against the tide, the whole Sound is a mass of confused and breaking seas. Then it is home only to the storm petrel.

PORTH OER

To cross from Bardsey Island to Braich y Pwll, and thence to Porth Oer, is a relatively simple matter on the flood. It sweeps you round the headland with pleasing swiftness, and then, running parallel with the coast of the Lleyn, it keeps pushing the kayak along. Off Braich y Pwll there is a tide race and rougher water, but this can be by-passed, if so desired, by sticking close in to the shore, for their are no strong counter-eddies to be avoided.

And so to Porth Oer, or Whistling Sands Bay, the last beach before (south of) the big headland of Penrhyn Mawr. Two stacks, Dinas Fawr and Dinas Fach, a kilometre south of the bay give warning of its approach. A road leads from the beach, and thence, by way of Carreg, back to Aberdaron. Alternatively there is a campsite two kilometres to the north above Porth Iago.

BARDSEY ISLAND

Finally a few words about the object of all this planning, Bardsey. Its Welsh name is *Ynys Enlli*, which means island in the currents. The Norsemen called it *Bards Eye*, the *eye* ending meaning *island,* as with Caldy, Ramsey and Lundy. The *Bards* were probably attracted to the Island during the Anglo-Saxon period because it had become famous as a holy place. In the sixth century the Pope declared that three pilgrimages to the Celtic monastery on Bardsey equalled one to Rome, and there is some archeological evidence to support the legend that 20,000 *saints* are buried on the Island. Certainly the need to cross Bardsey Sound a total of six times in hide covered rowing boats, cannot have increased their chances of returning home alive.

In the sixteenth and seventeenth centuries, after the dissolution of the monasteries, the Island became a base for pirates, and then, in the late nineteenth century, a small farming community grew up. Nothing remains of this except the sturdy farm buildings, now leased to bird watchers, the schoolroom, now a bird observatory, and a flock of sheep without a shepherd. Since 1971 no-one, except the lighthouse keepers if they are to be counted, has lived permanently on the Island.

Birdwatchers, and other visitors to the nature reserve of Bardsey Island, travel by boat every Saturday in the summer, weather permitting. About forty species of birds nest on the Island, safe from

An immature cormorant checks out some sea canoes.
Photo: Nigel Foster

the predation of man, as well as rats, foxes, and hedgehogs. Razorbills, Guillemots, Shags, Oyster-catchers, Kittiwakes, Manx Shearwaters, and Choughs are among the birds that can be seen here. Seals, porpoises and dolphins play around the Island, and lobster and mackerel are plentiful.

The lighthouse (Gp Fl S ev 15 secs, Vis 28M, Horn Mo N) is a tall square tower on Carn Duban - the name given to the southern part of Bardsey - about half a kilometre from the southern tip of the Island. Carn Duban is connected to the rest of the Island by a narrow isthmus, and this offers the best landing for canoeists; to the west is Porth Solfach, a small beach, and, even better, to the east is Cefn Enlli, a narrow gully which broadens into a shingle beach. A boathouse and slipway stand at the head of the gully. The main part of the Island to the north rises to a height of 167 metres (Mynedd Enlli), and this mountain drops sheer into the sea on the north and east making landing impossible.

Lleyn Peninsula, North Coast

Access: Porth Towyn (G.R.230374); or Morfa Nefyn (G.R.283408)
Distance: 19 kilometres; or 13 kilometres.
Max. Rate of Tidal Streams: 3 knots (springs), 2 knots (neaps).
Tide Race: Porth Dinllaen (G.R.276421)
Slack Water Constant: - 2.15
Duration of Slack: 0.30

Introduction

The paddle from Porth Towyn to Trevor along the north coast of the Lleyn Peninsula, is long in distance, but may be comfortably accomplished within one phase of the tide. There may be time to grab 'a swift half' in the pub at Porth Dinllaen, and with the tides and navigation being so straightforward - tidal streams between Towyn and Trevor run roughly parallel with the coast - 'erratic steerage' is not a problem. This technically easy trip will appeal to those looking for a long day along a deserted and varied coastline. A shorter version, from Porth Dinllaen to Trevor, takes in the best of the trip (for the less energetic), and is more sheltered from the prevailing south-westerly winds.

DINLLAEN

Between Porth Towyn - a popular surf beach after northerly winds - and Porth Dinllaen the coast is low and rocky. Landing on the headland of Trwyn Porth Dinllaen may be effected on the west or east coast, the latter being much more sheltered, and the site of a small harbour called Porth Dinllaen.

At the head of Porth Dinllaen stands a conspicuous red brick house, Ty Coch Inn, the most accessible canoeist's pub in North Wales. Half a kilometre to the north on the headland is the lifeboat station, housing the only lifeboat between Holyhead and Pwllheli. And one hundred metres to the north again is the extremity of the headland, off which a small tide race runs, most noticeable on the east-going flood stream.

After passing Trwyn Porth Dinllaen it is best, except in strong offshore winds, to keep out to sea. For, with the strength of the flood, the stream offsetting from the headland causes an eddy stream to set round Dinllaen Bay in a clockwise direction (a weaker anti-clockwise eddy occurs, on the ebb, to the west of the headland). In any event, if you are canoeing in the direction described, the coastline between Trwyn Porth Dinllaen and Penrhyn Glas (G.R.336439) is rather flat

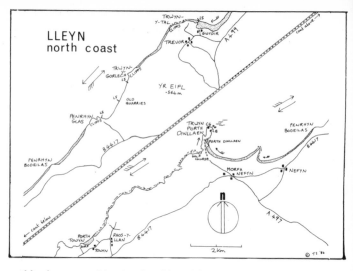

and boring, so nothing is missed by taking the direct route. Access for the shorter trip is at Morfa Nefyn, from a road running down to Porth Dinllaen beach.

CLIFFS, QUARRIES AND CAVES

By contrast, the coast beyond Penrhyn Glas is of great interest, both to the naturalist and archaeologist. It is littered with old quarry workings and their attendant buildings and jetties. A restored granite quarry hamlet, Nant Gwrtheyrn, is accessible from the sea, by a jetty south of Trwsyn y Gorlech (G.R.353452). There are two very steep headlands, the aforementioned Trwyn y Gorlech and Trwyn-y-Tal (G.R.3647). These are fronted by cliffs a hundred and fifty metres high, the home of puffins and guillemots, the more so because loose rock makes the area unattractive to climbers. Under Trwyn-y-Tal are some interesting caves with linking passages, best explored by landing on the beaches inside the caves and crawling along the holes!

And so to Trevor, and a concrete pier where stone was loaded. A rather unprepossessing end to such a scenic trip, you may think. Perhaps it is best to paddle on the ebb, and leave these industrial remains behind. But then this decision is not really the canoeist's to make, it being determined more by the workday demands of industrial society. Looked at in this way, the industrial archeology of concrete, granite, and iron is perhaps a useful reminder of the irony inherent in the canoeist's 'escape' to the sea.

Llandwyn Island

Access and Egress: Newborough Forest (G.R.405633)
Distance: 7 Kilometres
Max. Rate of Tidal Streams: 1½ knots (springs), ½ knot (neaps).
Overfalls and Tide Races: None
Slack Water Constant: - 1.50
Duration of Slack: 3.00 to 5.00

Introduction

Clear water, sunny beaches, isolated bays, these are the memories you will take away from Llandwyn Island. It is probably the most beautiful and secluded place on the Anglesey shore. There is little that is adventurous about this trip, but this is not a quality that will be missed. There is too much else; the mystery of derelict buildings, the peace of sandy coves, and nature in all its sea and coastal forms.

NEWBOROUGH

It is now possible to drive through Newborough village to a car park at the access point. Fortunately more than a kilometre of beach separates this point from Llandwyn Island, so although it is an easy paddle, it is too far for the deck chair brigade. Indeed it is worth remembering that the Island is a nature reserve, and any unnecessary intrusion upon the natural should be avoided.

LLANDWYN

Having paddled the kilometre along Newborough beach towards Llandwyn *Island*, you will wonder at that suffix, for, on all but high spring tides, there is a partly manufactured isthmus joining the Island to Anglesey. This isthmus must therefore be portaged on the outward or return journey to complete the circumnavigation of the Island.

Tides in the vicinity of Llandwyn Island are so weak as to be inconsequential for the canoeist. It matters little therefore, which way round you go, although a clockwise circumnavigation seems normal. Assuming this, the first notable feature is Pilots Cove which lies on the east shore towards the point of the Island. This affords full shelter from winds between west right round to north-east, and is therefore, a popular overnight stop for yachtsmen... and smugglers. Some years ago a million pounds worth of marijuana was seized from a boat anchored here!

At the southern entrance to Pilots Cove stands a ruined building which housed a lifeboat between 1840 and 1907. The crew were

93

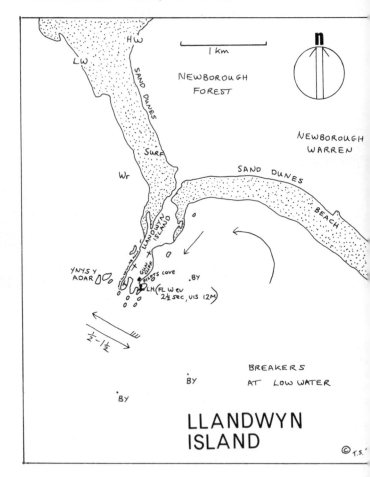

LLANDWYN
ISLAND

© T.S.

summoned from Newborough by firing a cannon. This cannon stands
there today, perched on 'Gun Cliff', its muzzle pointed out to sea.

There are two lighthouses on the tip of the Island. The eastern one,
which is above Pilots Cove, shows a white light out to sea, with a
shorter range red arc over the Caernarvon bar buoys (Fl W & R ev
2½s, vis 7M & 4M). The bigger western one was the original

94

Heading west off Llandwyn, with the hills of Snowdonia in the background. Photo: Derek Mayes

lighthouse. It is now abandoned, as are the Caernarvon pilots cottages close by. The latter however, have been restored and refurbished into a miniature museum, and are well worth a visit. Further exploration will reveal the ruins of an old monastery founded by St. Dwynwen in the sixth century. Two crosses are prominent close by.

The lee, or west shore, of Llandwyn, usually has a heavier swell running on it, due to the prevailing wind. It is often a good place therefore, to do some rock slalom. When this tires, there is always the spectacle of a thousand shags, guillemots, and gulls on and above Ynys y Adar. Running on to the sandy beach to the north-west of the Island, there is the chance of some good surf.

On a clear windless day however, there is only the wreck of a large fishing boat close inshore (visible at low water), to remind you that this is the Irish Sea and not some idyllic corner of the Aegean. Carrying the boats across the causeway you will not cross many tracks. So it may be with some regret that you paddle back towards Newborough Forest, the crowds, and the carpark.

Rhoscolyn

Access: Borthwen (G.R.272751)
Egress: Trearddur Bay (G.R.253790)
Distance: 7 kilometres
Max. Rate of Tidal Streams: 4 knots (springs), 2 knots (neaps)
Tide Races: Beacon Rocks, Maen y Fran, Rhoscolyn Head
Slack Water Constant: − 1.30 (− 3.00 Rhoscolyn Sound)
Duration of Slack: 0.30

Introduction

The paddle round Rhoscolyn and into Penrhos Bay is among the most appealing sea trips on Anglesey. The cliffs, while not as high and dramatic as those off the Stacks, are indented and cavernous, providing endless possibilities for the inquisitive paddler. The coast is littered with islets and islands, the former providing great sport in rock dodging, while the latter offer landings for bird watching and seal spotting. The tide races are strong enough on springs to warrant careful planning. And as a whole, Rhoscolyn is less frequented by people, whether it be the casual tourist, eager fisherman, or dedicated climber, than many other areas in this guide.

There is little to choose between starting at Borthwen or Trearddur Bay. This description begins at the former, because it seems marginally preferably to deal with the stronger tides off Rhoscolyn first - while mind and muscle are still fresh - and then to relax among the calmer bays of Penrhos. That said, it will, of course, be the time of slack water on the day that will determine that choice.

BORTHWEN

Finding and negotiating the tiny winding road from Rhoscolyn village to Borthwen is probably the crux of the whole trip for the first-timer. Once at Borthwen, a carpark and toilets abut conveniently onto the beach. The sea passage out of the south-western corner of Borthwen - past the old life-boat station and through the islands of Ynys Traws - is almost as narrow as the road in. A canoe wedged sideways here, after the down surge of the swell, can give the occupant an interesting exercise in deep air rolling.

RHOSCOLYN

Once through the islands at Borthwen's south-western entrance, the whole of the headland, with it's attendant islands, comes into view. Closest is Rhoscolyn Point (G.R.267746), and the off-lying Beacon

Rocks, with their distinctive white beacon and refuge (no light) on the offshore group (G.R.263741). Landing may be effected on Beacon Island from a channel on the south side. Seals are often seen here, while the largest inshore island hosts a cormorant colony.

One and half kilometres to the north-west is Rhoscolyn Head (G.R.256755), the highest point of land along this section of coastline. Between Rhoscolyn Point and Rhoscolyn Head, but nearer to the latter, lie three groups of islands named, respectively from south-east to north-west, Maen-y-Fran, Yr Henbont, and Maen-yr-Esgyll. Overlooking Maen-y-Fran is an auxiliary coastguard station, which is usually manned at weekends and in adverse weather (G.R.263751).

The numerous islands and indented coastline of Rhoscolyn cause local eddies close inshore and behind the islands, on both ebb and flood tides. On springs, the main stream can run at up to 4 knots, although 3½ knots is more usual. On the flood there is a tide race off the southern tip of Beacon Rocks, stretching for half a kilometre to the westward, and off the seaward end of Men-y-Fran, running for two or three hundred metres to the south-westward. The ebb stream causes a small tide race off Rhoscolyn Head, setting in a south south-westerly direction.

RHOSCOLYN SOUND

The area betwen Maen-y-Fran and Rhoscolyn Head, and bounded by the other above mentioned islands of Yr Henbont, and Maen-yr-Esgyll, called Rhoscolyn Sound, is worth considering in a little more detail. Here the inshore stream changes an hour and half early, due, no doubt, to the offset, on the flood, from Maen-y-Fran, and on the ebb, from Rhoscolyn Head. The north-westerly flow of the tidal stream in Rhoscolyn Sound, up to an hour and half before low water, is particularly noticeable. After low water, the same inshore westerly stream has enough strength to cause localised eddies behind the islands in the Sound, and behind Rhoscolyn Head in Penrhos Bay. These eddies circulate in a clockwise direction.

Added to the peculiar tidal streams in Rhoscolyn Sound, there are flukey winds. These are probably produced by the exceptionally flat headland, which offers no resistance to offshore winds and draughts. All of which should not put you off paddling into The Dungeon, a vast and obvious cave, just before you round the headland into Penrhos Bay.

PENRHOS BAY

The coastline between Rhoscolyn Head and Trearddur Bay seems to be made for pottering. The first cove is Porth Saint, with a boulder strewn beach difficult to land on. Three quarters of a kilometre, and a kilometre to the north, respectively, are White Arch and Black Arch, both stupendous pieces of rock architecture, which can only be visited by canoe or rowing boat. Many a classic sea-canoeing photograph has been taken here.

Porth-y-Cromlech, or Smuggler's Cove, is about a half kilometre to the north again, and has an entrance only a few metres wide, and that only at high water. Porth-y-Garan, or Waterlily Cove, half a kilometre still further on, is slightly larger, and offers a shingle beach for landing. The attractively named Deadman's Cove is the distinctive narrow inlet facing north-westward a quarter of a kilometre to the north. Ravenspoint (G.R.250779) marks the northern end of this fascinating section of coastline, and has reefs to the north and south which offer good sport in a swell. And beyond Ravenspoint is Trearddur Bay, dry clothes and ice-cream.

Out of the darkness and into the sun: The Dungeon in Rhoscolyn Sound.
Photo: Derek Mayes

Penrhyn Mawr

Access: Trearddur Bay (G.R.253790)
Egress: Abrahams Bosom (G.R.215814)
Distance: 7 kilometres
Max. Rate of Tidal Streams: 5 knots (springs), 3 knots (neaps)
Overfalls and Tide Race: Penrhyn Mawr
Slack Water Constant: High Water -1.15   Low Water - c.2.30
Duration of Slack: 0.30

Introduction

Penrhyn Mawr shares, with North Stack, the reputation of having the wildest water off the North Wales Coast. In point of fact, the overfalls in Bardsey Sound and off the Skerries are just as big, but Penrhyn Mawr's and North Stack's ease of access have spread their fame beyond that of their more serious counterparts. Certainly Penrhyn Mawr is a spectacular sight (from the headland!) in heavy weather, but in light winds the waves here will not frighten the competent roller or well-led party.

It is worth then, going on the strength of the flood, when the roller-coaster is running. This is the direction taken by the following description. An hour's play in the middle of the trip seems a just counter-point to the more leisurely exploration of the rugged and indented coastline between Trearddur Bay on the one side, and Abrahams Bosom on the other.

PENRHOS BAY

It is the offset from the Stacks on the ebb which makes a trip round Penrhyn Mawr, on that tide, less exciting. Indeed this ebb stream, running in a south-westerly direction off the Stacks, sets up an eddy in Penrhos Bay which the canoeist can use to start from there, on the last of that tide. Access in Trearddur Bay is from a parking area next to the beach. For a shorter trip, it is best to start at Porth Dafarch (G.R.233799), where there is also parking onto the beach. At Porth Dafarch a ruined quay and customs house are reminders of the days before steam, when sailing packets used the bay to shelter from adverse winds round the Stacks.

A kilometre further west, but still in Penrhos Bay, is Porth Rhuffydd (G.R.217798), where an old lifeboat station is squeezed between steep cliffs above a pebble beach. A narrow footpath leads to a good track and the road a kilometre to the north. A favourite place for the air-sea rescue helicopters from R.A.F. Valley to practice, it is the best lunch spot for those who have used the eddy stream, and are waiting for the flood to get going off Penrhyn Mawr. The rocky cliffs stretching out from either side of the bay offer good sea-level traverses for any rock stars, and an investigation of the caves and inlets to the south may be rewarded by a close encounter with seals.

PENRHYN MAWR

Penrhyn Mawr, or Penrhos Point, is a triple pointed headland forming the northern tip of Penrhos Bay, and the southern tip of Abrahams Bosom. Stretching for a kilometre southward off the southern extremity of the headland are two groups of small islands through which the tide races. The larger northern group of islets, lying close to the headland, are known as Tide Rip Rocks, while those smaller ones further offshore are known as The Fangs.

During the strength of the flood tide, the inshore stream, setting to the north-westwards, runs past Penrhyn Mawr at up to 5 knots on springs and 3 knots on neaps. This forms a tide race with heavy overfalls from Tide Rip Rocks and the Fangs to a point about half a mile off the western extremity of the headland. The rough water is well-defined in chutes and streams, and the return eddies are within easy reach, so excellent sport may be had here. In north-westerly or westerly winds however, the flood stream kicks up very rough, and the canoeist may prefer to sneak between Tide Rip Rocks and the headland. It is also possible to sneak this passage against the flood tide, if coming from Abrahams Bosom. Indeed for the first one and a half hours of the flood (see below for details) the stream close inshore to the headland is still ebbing, for *it* changes at roughly the same time as Low Water in the area.

On the ebb, the stream is much weaker, due to the offset from the Stacks. In fact, the north going eddies in Penrhos Bay and Abrahams Bosom on the ebb, encourages the main stream (and hence the overfalls) to start running north-west well before Low Water - most observers agree that it is between one and two hours before. This means that the flood stream, through Tide Rip Rocks and The Fangs runs most strongly in the first two hours after Low Water - because *Slack* Water (Low) is about one and a half hours earlier. Here then is another example of a tidal anomaly. The stream round Penrhyn Mawr floods for about seven hours and ebbs for about five.

ABRAHAMS BOSOM

Tidal streams in Abrahams Bosom are fairly weak, but eddy in opposition to the main stream. This is particularly noticeable at the southern end of the bay on the flood. The best beach for access and egress is in the northernmost of the three bays, the southern half of which provides a steep and muddy cliff path out on to the South Stack road. This rather harrowing carry is made worse at low tide by a boulder strewn foreshore. Few, however, will mind much about slippery seaweed at the end of a trip such as this.

The Stacks

Access: Soldiers Point (G.R.236837)
Egress: Abrahams Bosom (G.R.215814)
Distance: 7 kilometres
Max. Rate of Tidal Streams: 6 knots (springs), 3 knots (neaps)
Overfalls and Tide Races: North Stack, South Stack
Slack Water Constant: North Stack H.W.-2.00, L.W.-1.00;
   South Stack H.W. & L.W. -1.10
Duration of Slack: 0.30

Introduction

The western extremities of Anglesey, which are called The Stacks, together with the western extremities of the Lleyn and Pembroke peninsulars, are the outposts of Wales in the Irish Sea. As such, they receive the most of storm and tide, the highest of wind and wave, and their cliffs are the least hospitable to man. Sandwiched between the hammer of the sea, and anvil of the rugged schists and gneisses, the sea canoeist can pay dearly for an error in planning, or a misjudgement of conditions. But if the risks are there, so are the rewards - stupendous rock architecture, seabirds in profusion (fulmars, shags, puffins, guillemots, razorbills, gannets, and sometimes, in later summer, artic skua), inquisitive seals, huge waves to play in, strong currents to carry you, and, above all, the feeling of commitment, for once started there is no easy escape.

Tide Races and Overfalls

The seriousness of the Stacks trip is compounded by the presence of overfalls and exceptionally strong tidal streams. Overfalls lie just north of North Stack and west of South Stack. The tidal stream, running at 6 knots on springs and 3 to 4 knots on neaps across these overfalls, causes a confused and breaking sea extending for between one and two kilometres off the shore. North Stack overfalls run mainly on the ebb, South Stack overfalls on the flood. On the strength of the tide, and when wind is opposed to tide, the waves here can be very big.

The tide races and overfalls are described in the Admiralty Pilot as being 'dangerous for boats'. Certainly for those chary of big water, a passage round the Stacks at, or near, Slack Water is recommended. The alternative is to sneak between the Stacks and the cliffs avoiding the main tide races, but this is not always possible in rough conditions. A number of parties have become unstuck in these races due to multiple capsizes. The opposing effects of wind and tide can quickly separate boat from swimmer, who is then difficult to spot in the

Exploring caves and passages near South Stack.
Photo: Derek Mayes

troughs. This is not a good way to see Ireland! Having said that, the experienced slalom or sea canoeist will find good sport in these huge waves, a welcome change from the monotony of flat water paddling.

Tidal Streams

The main tidal stream off the Stacks, sets north-east with the flood and south-west with the ebb. The stream, with one important exception (the ebb off North Stack), changes direction at approximately the same time as High and Low Water in the area. For North Stack this is about ten minutes before Holyhead harbour, and, for South Stack, about twenty minutes before (high and low water Holyhead is measured at the entrance to the Inner Harbour). Thus the flood stream starts running north-east off South Stack twenty minutes before L.W. Holyhead, and off North Stack (further out to sea) ten minutes before, while the ebb stream starts running south-west off South Stack twenty minutes before H.W. Holyhead. This is based on my own observations, but there is some difference of opinion regarding the exact timings - See Glazebrook and The Admiralty Pilot.

The exception to the above is the timing of the ebb stream between Holyhead and North Stack and off North Stack itself (and hence also the overfalls). This starts running west an *hour* before H.W. Holyhead, probably because of the eddying effect of the flood stream in Holyhead Bay. Whatever the cause, the result is that North Stack tide race is running *heavily* south-west shortly after H.W. Holyhead, and starts to die away three hours later.

The strong tidal streams cause local eddies to be set up in the lee of North and South Stack on the flood, and in the lee of North Stack on the ebb. For a fast journey in the middle hours of the tide therefore, the canoeist should keep out of Gogarth Bay, and thus benefit from the mainstream. Most however, will want to take a close look at the cliffs, caves and passages here, even if it means fighting the eddy. Let us therefore, return to a description of the trip and points of interest along the way.

SOLDIERS POINT

The choice of direction will, of course, be determined by the state of the tide on the day, so this anti-clockwise description is arbitrary. Soldiers Point and Port Namarch (G.R.225834) both provide convenient access points. A tarmac road leads from Holyhead to the former, and an old quarry railway track (driveable) continues on to the latter. At Soldiers Point it is worth starting west of the breakwater, otherwise a rather tedious and unnecessary four kilometres is added to the trip.

Annie's Arch in Gogarth Bay. Photo:Derek Mayes

NORTH STACK

North Stack is quickly reached from Porth Namarch, the stack itself being separated from the projecting spur of Holyhead Mountain by a fifty foot wide gully. On top of this one hundred and fifty foot high spur are the white buildings of the Fog Warning Station (Horn 3). Beneath its west flank is the huge Parliament House Cave (G.R.214839), so named because of the great assembly of seabirds which gather there, making an incessant chatter as if in the process of some mighty debate concerning future policy.

On all but high spring tides, there is a strip of pebble beach exposed under that mighty roof, three hundred feet wide and one hundred feet long, surely the most dramatic lunch or bivy spot in North Wales. A dark and watery tunnel, too tight for canoes but admitting a person, leads from the corner of the cavern to the north side of the spur, and so, by way of scrambling, to the North Stack Fog Warning Station. One group at least, on waking from a stormy bivouac, have been grateful for this narrow escape route! Exposed among the rocks that litter the approach to the cave at low tide are massive iron cannons, used as fog signals before the Station was built.

South Stack lighthouse from the south.   Photo Derek Mayes

GOGARTH BAY

Proceeding in the direction of South Stack, the canoeist, who keeps inshore, will be able to pass through *Annie's Arch*, and then under *Wen Slab*, where goes the famous climb *A Dream of White Horses*. All along these sea cliffs, appropriately named *Gogarth* by climbers, there will, on a summer's day, be ropes, cries of 'safe', and silent struggles with the rock. This encounter gives canoeist and climber alike, a chance to relax in mutual incredulity at the other's sport.

SOUTH STACK

South Stack is a much larger island than its northern cousin, and is joined to the mainland by a pedestrian suspension bridge. It is topped by a lighthouse (Fl W ev 10s, Vis 20M, occas. Fixed R Light, Horn 1 ev 30s), a round white painted tower with lightkeepers houses surrounding it. This light is due to go automatic, but, as I write, still welcomes visitors.

Once round South Stack, or through South Stack gully, and only a canoe can go that way, Penlas Rock, and in the distance Penrhyn Mawr, come into view. Penlas Rock (G.R.207815) is a large limestone stack apparently attached, but, in fact, detached from the main cliff, a

Heading south out of South Stack Gully
Photo: Derek Mayes

kilometre south of South Stack. The intervening cliffs are home to nesting birds in season, particularly auks - paddlers should keep out to sea in this period, February to July - and out of season to climbers, particularly good ones. The latter have named the cliffs from north to south, *Mousetrap Zawn* (this first cliff round from South Stack looks like, and has the consistency of Swiss cheese), *Red Wall, Castell Helen* (Ellin's Tower, a nineteenth century summer house converted into a bird watching centre, stands on top), and finally *Yellow Wall.* The rock then degenerates towards Penlas, but there remain some great little passages for the canoeist.

ABRAHAMS BOSOM

Round from Penlas Rock is Abrahams Bosom, a deep bay marking the end of the trip. A beach in the north-eastern corner of the bay has a steep path leading to the cliff top, and thence to the South Stack Road. Lest however, it's name, or the prospect of landing there, lead you into too false a sense of security, the Biblical sense of Abrahams Bosom is 'the repose of the happy in death'. This is an indication of the number of wrecks listed here. But there also seems to be a fair amount of fibre glass and polystyrene littering the beach!

Circumnavigation of Holy Island

Access and Egress: Four Mile Bridge (G.R.280783), Stanley
Embankment (G.R.281801), Soldiers Point (G.R.236837), Porth
Namarch (G.R.225834), Abrahams Bosom (G.R.215814), Porth
Dafarch (G.R.233799), Borthwen (G.R.272751)
Distance: c.32 kilometres
Max. Rate of Tidal Streams: 6 knots (springs), 4 knots (neaps)
Overfalls and Tide Races: Holyhead Breakwater, North Stack,
South Stack, Penrhyn Mawr, Rhoscolyn
Stack Water Constants: Holyhead - 1.00; Rhoscolyn - 1.30; Inland
Sea H.W. + 1.00, L.W. + 2.00 (see also Stacks and Penrhyn
Mawr).
Duration of Slack: Holyhead and Rhoscolyn 0.30; Inland Sea 0.10
(springs), 0.30 (neaps)

Introduction

The circumnavigation of Holy Island provides one of the most exciting
and challenging trips in North Wales. Strong tidal streams, overfalls,
sheer cliffs and intricate tidal calculations, all combine to make a
successful trip round the island a notable event in anyone's diary.

The point of departure and arrival depends entirely on the state of
the tide and your personal predilection. Some will want to use the
strength of the tide round the Stacks to give a swift passage, while
others will prefer a slower and calmer paddle near Slack Water. It
must be borne in mind however, that entry *and* exit from the Inland
Sea is only possible near Slack Water. A true circumnavigation
(without portage) is most easily achieved therefore, by planning the
trip round the state of the tide at Stanley Embankment and Four Mile
Bridge.

This description takes an anti-clockwise direction round Holy
Island. This is purely arbitrary since the decision to go clockwise or
anti-clockwise is most likely to be taken on the basis of the time of
Slack Water in the Inland Sea on the day. It is however, advisable to
traverse the Inland Sea early on, since *precise* timing here is more
crucial than on any other part of the trip.

If Slack Water High is in the morning, a clockwise circumnavigation
starting in Holyhead Harbour an hour before Slack Water (Inland
Sea) allows the canoeist to take advantage of the ebb in the Cymran
Strait. If Slack Water Low is in the morning, an anti-clockwise paddle
starting and finishing at Four Mile Bridge allows the Cymran Strait to
be done on the flood at the end of the trip. It will become apparent, as

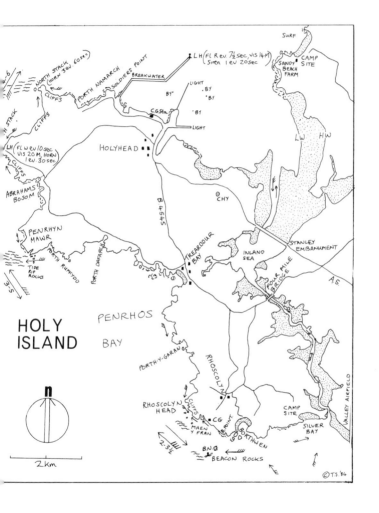

HOLY ISLAND

PENRHOS BAY

n

2km

you plan the trip, that a leisurely circumnavigation in either direction will mean stopping at the entrance to the Cymran Strait or at Borthwen to wait for the tide to turn to your advantage.

While the Inland Sea constitutes the crux of the trip in terms of tidal planning, the Stacks, Penrhyn Mawr, and Rhoscolyn are the most committing sections of coastline to canoe. Should someone become separated from their canoe in these areas, swimming is not going to do a lot of good. It should be noted therefore that these three areas are dealt with in much greater detail elsewhere in the guide - separate trips in fact. It will be well worth reading these descriptions before planning the circumnavigation.

THE INLAND SEA

Four Mile Bridge marks the northern end of the Cymran Strait, which, with the Inland Sea, divides Holy Island from Anglesey. The Inland Sea is formed by Four Mile Bridge in the south and by Stanley Embankment in the north, and extends for a distance of one and half miles between them. Water flows in and out of the Inland Sea through two tunnels, one in the Bridge and the other in the Embankment. These tunnels are approximately ten feet wide and five feet high, the one in Stanley Embankment being longer. Such is the pressure of water in these tunnels that passage against all but the first and last half hour of the tide is impossible.

The surge of water through the tunnels produces an excellent playground for those wishing to practice white water techniques. Four Mile Bridge has a particularly good shoot of moving water on the flood. Stanley Embankment however, is dangerous at certain states of the tide. At the height of the ebb a vicious canoe gobbling stopper develops on the seaward side of the Embankment, and on the flood a stopper forms *inside* the tunnel. This powerful hidden stopper, which is closed off at both sides, has been known to back-loop sea kayaks, and will be the death of someone someday. It has already caused one good paddler to sell his boat and give up canoeing entirely.

The length of the Cymran Strait - four miles - means that the flood takes about three hours to arrive at Four Mile Bridge after Low Water at Holyhead. The flood only takes an hour to reach Stanley Embankment from the other side, but because a three foot ramp has been built into this tunnel (the cause of the stopper wave) another two hours is needed before it will start flooding into the Inland Sea. This is why Slack Water Low in the Inland Sea is about three hours after Slack Water Low at Holyhead. Once the flood starts to run in at both ends, the amount of water in the Inland Sea quickly builds up until after five hours no more can enter. Thus Slack Water High is two hours after High Water at Holyhead.

It must be admitted that apart from this fascinating tidal anomaly and the exciting white water spouts at either end, there is little to recommend the Inland Sea to the canoeist. Once clear of Stanley Embankment however, the Irish Sea, in all it's moods, soon makes itself felt. Indeed the paddle to Holyhead Harbour may be enlivened by quite a choppy sea, if the wind is in the northern quadrant.

HOLYHEAD BAY

There are in reality two harbours at Holyhead. There is the Old Harbour guarded by Salt Island (G.R.2583), and used by the ferries to Ireland, and there is the New Harbour guarded by a breakwater one and a half miles long with a black and white lighthouse at the end (Fl R ev 7½s, vis 14M, Siren I ev 20s). These harbours are divided by Salt Island and by its extension the Rio Tinto Zinc jetty, from which aluminium powder is taken by conveyor belt to a refining plant on the other side of Holyhead (the chimney of this plant provides one of the most useful transit points for canoeists paddling round Holy Island). The area inside the New Harbour is fairly sheltered, except in north-easterly winds. There is probably no truth to the story that the designer of the breakwater threw himself off the end as he watched the first north-easterly gale blow straight in, but it certainly seems as though the curves have been put in the wrong way round!

If you left Stanley Embankment at slack water high, you may be surprised at the strength of the ebb tide in Holyhead Bay; for the inshore stream near the breakwater begins to set westwards as far as North Stack an hour before High Water Holyhead (the east going stream or flood is not so strong and begins shortly after Low Water Holyhead). This early start of the ebb is worth remembering if you plan to come round the Stacks on the flood, for if you are late it may well add half an hour to your paddle across the bay. Even more important it means that the North Stack tide race, which is a monster on the ebb, starts to run west *an hour before High Water at Holyhead.*

There is a small tide race off the end of the breakwater on the ebb, and there can be considerable clapotis on the west side if the wind is from that direction. Between it and North Stack there are (at the time of writing) two road access points, Soldiers Point on the landward end of the breakwater, and further west, Porth Namarch. Five kilometres of rugged coastline without good landfall lie between Porth Namarch and the next point of egress, so this is a good place for second thoughts.

THE WEST COAST

The trip round North and South Stack is described in greater detail elsewhere in this guide. Suffice it to say that there are strong tide races off both North Stack (G.R.213839) and South Stack (G.R.201822) running at up to 6 knots on springs. Moreover there are overfalls off both Stacks, which, combined with the races, causes a confused, steep, and breaking sea. Things can get pretty mean around these headlands, particularly if there is an opposing wind.

Once round South Stack or through South Stack Gully - and only a canoe can go that way - Penrhyn Mawr comes into view. Between the two headlands lies Abrahams Bosom, a deep bay which affords access to the South Stack road by way of a very steep path. This would be a good place to pull out if the weather has turned, for Penrhyn Mawr is not a good place to be in rough conditions. On the strength of the spring flood tide the overfalls off Penrhyn Mawr produce wild water only equalled on the Anglesey coast by that off North Stack on the ebb. Penrhyn Mawr and the attendant coastline is described in detail elsewhere in this guide, and reference should be made to it.

The same applies to Rhoscolyn, the last major headland on the circumnavigation - it is treated separately as a shorter trip, and reference should be made to that description. Between Penrhyn Mawr and Rhoscolyn, there is the long flog across Penrhos Bay. This bay is the home of strong eddies due to the offsetting of the ebb stream from Penrhyn Mawr, and the offsetting of the flood stream from Rhoscolyn, so for those going with the tide in either direction it is best to keep well out to sea on this six kilometre crossing.

The Beacon rocks off Rhoscolyn with their distinctive white tower (no light) beckon from afar, and once there offer a landing in calm weather. Better still there is Borthwen just round the corner, a secluded sandy beach of derelict slipways and great charm. A narrow and impossibly windy road affords access to the north-west corner of the beach.

THE CYMRAN STRAIT

For the circumnavigator, Rhoscolyn is the last major obstacle before the lazy tides and low sandy foreshore of Holy Island's south coast. Little now stands between you and the circumnavigation of the Island, except fatigue and the Cymran Strait. It would be a shame if these two became synonymous, for the Strait is a beautiful unspoilt strip of water. So keep some energy to savour this place, and avoid battling the stream, it can flow at 4 knots on the stronger ebb. At low water you will have it entirely to yourself, since no other craft can navigate the narrow channel. Where the channel divides take the left hand branch, and within ten minutes you will be back at Four Mile Bridge. But be warned, the boys digging for worms below the High Water mark will hardly acknowledge your presence, let alone help your tired limbs drag the boat across the sucking mud.

Caving by kayak in Penrhos Bay.
Photo: Derek Mayes

The Skerries

Access and Egress: Abrahams Bosom (G.R.215814), or Porth Swtan (G.R.300891), or Cemlyn Bay (G.R.329935)

Distance: Return trip from: Abrahams Bosom   30 kilometres
                                    Porth Swtan   14 kilometres
                                    Cemlyn   15 kilometres

Max. Rate of Tidal Streams: 6 knots (springs), 3 knots (neaps)

Tide Races and Overfalls: Harry Furlong's Rocks, Carmel Head, Carmel Rocks, East Platters, West Platters, Langdon Ridge

Slack Water Constant: Coastal (eg. West Mouse) −0.45
                            Offshore (eg. Skerries) -1.15
                            Carmel Head H.W.S. -1.15; L.W.S. -2.15

Duration of Slack: 0.20

Introduction

The Skerries is one of the classic sea canoeing trips of North Wales. It is a committing offshore paddle to an island in the middle of the main Irish Sea tidal stream. It requires detailed tidal planning, not to mention good technique to deal with the overfalls that surround the Island. The Skerries themselves are barren and inhospitable compared to Bardsey, but the coastal scenery on the way could hardly be bettered.

ABRAHAMS BOSOM AND LANGDON RIDGE

The most adventurous route to the Skerries (apart from over the Irish Sea) is across Holyhead Bay from Abrahams Bosom. On the strength of a spring flood (6 knots), this is much faster than the distance (15 kilometres) would suggest. After passing close to South Stack the paddler should leave North Stack a few hundred metres off to the east, and then also leave Langdon Ridge off to the right.

Langdon Ridge is a shelf of rock some 7 kilometres north of Soldiers Point, and 6 kilometres west of Porth Swtan. Being only nine metres under, it often produces an area of rougher water. It is marked by a black banded yellow buoy showing a white light at night (Very. Qk. Fl. 9 ev. 10 sec.). If you should pass to the right of this buoy (instead of to the left as recommended above), you will tend to be swept south of the Skerries through Carmel Head Gap as the flood stream turns east along the north coast of Anglesey.

Another good test of your position in Holyhead Bay, is the bearing of North Stack on South Stack. If, looking over your shoulder as you paddle towards the Skerries, the Stacks are in line, the same course

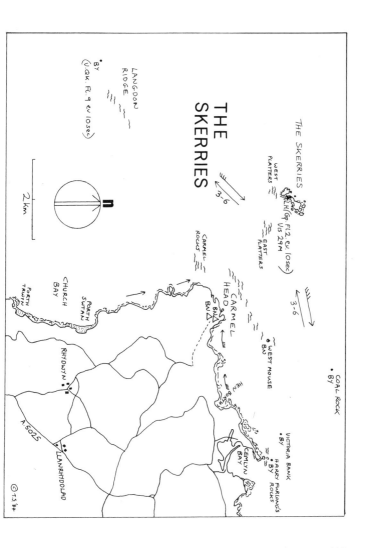

Umnak, Nordkapp, and Anas Acuta, off the Skerries.
Photo: Derek Mayes

(31 degrees) will take you almost directly *between* Carmel Head and the Skerries. So to make landfall on the Skerries, South Stack needs to be visible well out from North Stack.

It is harder to miss land on the return trip. There is always however, a tendency for the west going stream (ebb) to take the canoeist out to sea. So, when making for Holy Island, it is worth passing close to Langdon Ridge and then keeping North and South Stack roughly in line. Obviously this open sea crossing becomes much more serious in poor visibility. Not only may a compass be necessary, but also some very nifty paddling - the Irish ferry passes between Langdon Ridge and North Stack! Ferry sailing times are available from Holyhead Coastguard.

PORTH SWTAN

The route from Porth Swtan to the Skerries is much shorter. It does however, have its problems. Going on the flood it is necessary to head almost due west at first lest you pick up the north going stream too far north and it sweeps you through Carmel Head Gap. The flood stream runs most strongly about two kilometres offshore from Porth Swtan. Once in it, the canoeist will quickly bear down on the Skerries.

116

On some states of the tide it is possible to go directly north from Porth Swtan. An inshore north-going eddy stream is produced in the lee of Carmel Head by the ebb. So it is possible to use the last of this inshore eddy stream as far as Carmel Head, and then to cross to the Skerries on Slack Water. This is slower than the other options, and the tidal planning is fairly tight. The paddler must then wait for the flood to run its course, if he is returning to Porth Swtan.

On the return journey it is best to keep well out to sea until almost parallel with Porth Swtan - recognisable by its steep yellow cliffs, and not be be confused with its southerly neighbour Borthwen (rows of bungalows). This is because the inshore stream between Church Bay and Carmel Head sets to the north for about nine hours out of the twelve - a combination of the flood, and the ebb eddy mentioned above. This eddy runs from about one hour after High Water to about one hour before Low Water - the most likely interval for a return journey.

CEMLYN BAY

Although a combination of access and egress from different points makes the best of the Skerries trip, there is no doubt that, in terms of tidal planning, a trip to and from Cemlyn is the easiest. In distance, it is about half that from Abrahams Bosom and about equal to that from Porth Swtan; but the judgement of position in relation to the Skerries is easier and less crucial than on either of the other two routes. The paddle from Cemlyn still has a 'next stop Ireland' feel about it, but at least from here there is the coast nearby, and a couple of rocky islets, to give the illusion of safety.

Cemlyn is the most deserted major beach on Anglesey. There are no buildings, no moorings, no quay, and no warehouses, only an old lifeboat station between the sea and a strange still lagoon. By contrast the huge Wylfa Head Nuclear Power Station pulsates with unnatural life two kilometres to the east. At night two fixed green lights are shown off a jetty at the power station, visible from the west.

Harry Furlong's Rocks are the first feature out to sea from Cemlyn, lying close northward from Trwyn Cemlyn, the low north-western point of the bay. These are incorrectly named Harry *Furlough's* rocks on the O.S. map, the true name deriving from the belief that they were a furlong (220 yards) in length. They are in fact about two furlongs long; 'Harry' was obviously short-sighted. A green conical buoy marks the end of the reef. Tidal streams run strongly off this northern end, particularly on the ebb, and there are overfalls here. The rough water however, can be avoided on the landward side.

117

Continuing on towards the Skerries, Victoria Bank Buoy (black above yellow) is left to the north, and then West Mouse marks the half-way point and the last useful landfall before the Skerries. As an islet it is without interest, but the white beacon on it aligns with the 'White Ladies' - two ten metre high white stone pyramidal beacons on Carmel Head - on a bearing of 198 degrees to indicate the postion of Coal Rock Buoy (yellow above black) some two kilometres further out to sea. These four transit points offer the canoeist a useful way of judging position and speed, on both ebb and flood.

Overfalls

Whether approaching from Cemlyn or Holyhead Bay, the canoeist will almost certainly encounter rough water close to the Skerries. Tide rips and overfalls are concentrated around the Platters, two groups of off-lying rocks close to the Skerries. The East Platters are on the natural route from Cemlyn, since they lie half a kilometre south-eastward from the lighthouse. They dry to 4 feet on low water springs, and cause overfalls on both flood and ebb. The West Platters are most likely to be encountered by those coming from Holyhead Bay, since they extend for two hundred metres off the south-western extremity of the Skerries. They dry to 6 feet on low water springs, and cause a tide race and very big overfalls on both flood and ebb. They also help to create the strong inshore eddy stream, which may be found on the flood, running south-west close to the south shore of the Skerries.

A tide race, with overfalls, also develops off Carmel Head on both flood and ebb, but this area of rough water need not be crossed by the canoeist visiting the Skerries. To use the strength of the tidal stream to and from Cemlyn, a passage out to sea - well away from Carmel Head - is necessary. This is particularly true when returning to Cemlyn on the flood, for an eddy stream develops in the lee of Carmel Head close inshore between the headland and Henborth. It is worth remembering, too, that, out to sea (in the region of Coal Rock for instance), the tidal stream turns half an hour earlier than the inshore stream, so it picks up that much quicker. Finally, for those going round Carmel Head, note that here, the flood stream runs for seven hours while the ebb runs for just five.

THE SKERRIES

Well, what of the object of all this attention, the Skerries. They are a group of islets, divided by narrow gullies, about a kilometre in length on their longer axis which lies north-east to south-west. The western extremity of the group consists of a large stack called Ynys Arw, which is separated from the main islet by a long gully running north and south.

The northern end of this gully is known as the lagoon. It is the most sheltered place on the Skerries, and the best for landing. The southern entrance to the lagoon is narrow and dries at low water, but the northern entrance, within the sheltering arms of large rocks, is always clear. The lighthouse lies just above the lagoon, with a stone jetty and landing steps leading to it. This lighthouse (Gp Fl ev 10sec, Vis 17M; F.R. Vis 16M; Diaphone 2) is the most important on the North Wales coast, standing guard over the main shipping route into Liverpool.

The lighthouse is going automatic in 1986, so there will be no more cups of tea for the inquisitive or weary sea canoeist. Once more the Skerries will be the sole preserve of sea birds, seals and crustaceans. And that quiet breed of men whose self-sufficiency found a natural home in the loneliness of lighthouse keeping, must now look elsewhere for their employment.

The Skerries Lighthouse from the east.
Photo: Derek Mayes

Anglesey North Coast

Access: Amlwch (G.R.450934); or Bull Bay (G.R.426942).
Egress: Cemaes (G.R.369936)
Distance: 9 kilometres; or 7 kilomtres.
Max.Rate of Tidal Streams: 5 knots (springs), 3 knots (neaps).
Tide Races: East Mouse, Trwyn Melyn, Middle Mouse, Dinas Gynfor.
Slack Water Constant: Coastal - 0.50, Offshore -1.20
Duration of Slack: 0.30

Introduction

The north coast of Anglesey is one of contrasts. There are the 500,000 ton oil tankers moored two miles offshore discharging crude oil at the Amlwch oil terminal, while in Bull and Cemaes Bays there are tiny fishing boats struggling to maintain an essentially nineteenth century living. Beyond Cemaes, there is a power station imposing its artificial life upon Wylfa Head, while tide and wind rush, as yet untamed, along the sea outside. Still, above all, there is more of bird, sea and cliff, than anything else, which is as it should be for the sea canoeist. For him, or her, nature needs no helping hand along this section of coastline, to provide either interest or excitement.

AMLWCH

Amlwch is a good access point for the canoeist wanting to paddle the north coast of Anglesey. Until 1976 Amlwch was little more than a derelict memorial to the days of sail. Its prosperity in the eighteenth and nineteenth centuries was based on the copper mines of Parys Mountain two miles inland. Another cargo taken out of the port was Amlwch Shag, a chewing tobacco soaked in rum, very popular amongst the slate miners of North Wales.

Today the port is again a hive of activity due to the arrival of the oil terminal buoy two miles offshore, connected to Amlwch by submarine cable. Because of tankers manoeuvering in the vicinity, unauthorised navigation is prohibited within two thousand feet of the buoy. It nevertheless provides a useful 'landmark' for canoeists in fog, or indeed at night, when it is the only lighted point between the Skerries and Point Lynas, and very brightly lit at that (Light Mo U ev 15 sec, Horn Mo U ev 30 sec).

The best access point for canoeists in Amlwch is a slipway on the east side of the port, reached by following the harbour road through the village to its end. The trip as described here, goes from east to

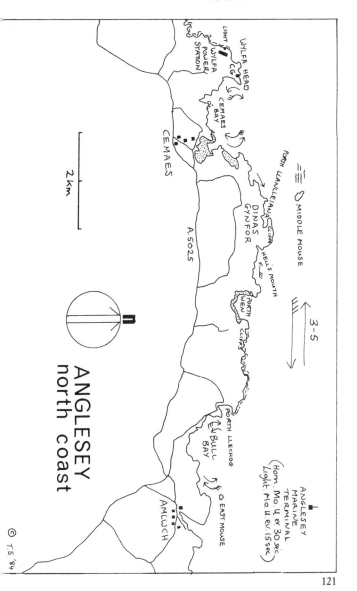

ANGLESEY
north coast

2 km

© T.S. '84

WYLFA HEAD
LIGHT
Gp
WYLFA POWER STATION
CEMAES BAY
CEMAES
A.5025
DINAS GYNFOR
PORTH LLANLLEIANA CLIFFS
HELL'S MOUTH
PORTH WEN
CLIFFS
PORTH LLECHOG
BULL BAY
PORTH LLECHOG
AMLWCH

MIDDLE MOUSE

3-5

EAST MOUSE

ANGLESEY MARINE TERMINAL
(Horn. Mo.U. ev.30.sec
Light. Mo.U.ev.15.sec)

west, and is best done on the ebb. To paddle on the flood from Cemaes is equally plausible, and it is possible, although more strenuous, to paddle against the first or last hours of the tidal stream by using the eddies and slack water close inshore.

BULL BAY

The first obvious landmark as you leave Amlwch is East Mouse, a rocky islet lying two hundred metres offshore. A passage inside East Mouse avoids the main tidal stream which, on springs, runs at least three knots here; but it also brings you within sniffing distance of the chemical works on the point. Tide rips run off the island on springs, due to underwater ledges.

Round the corner is Bull Bay, a tiny fishing port less spoilt than its neighbour. The Bay has strong eddies of up to two knots on both flood and ebb tides, so it is best avoided by the canoeist going with the stream. However, Porth Llechog, at the north-west tip of the bay, provides a good access point for those wanting a shorter trip along the north coast. A road conveniently runs right down to the beach.

PORTH WEN

The headland west of Bull Bay, called Trwyn Melyn, is rocky and precipitous, devoid of good landing. There is a tide rip off the eastern end of the headland. Two kilometres to the west is Porth Wen, a large bay half a kilometre square. A disused brickworks on the west side of the cove has a small shingle beach close by, with a path running down to it from the road half a kilometre away. The old kilns in the brickworks provide good bivouac shelters (G.R.401945). As a point of interest, the post on the headland to the west of Port Wen is one end of a measured nautical mile, the other end being marked by the post on the headland to the west of Porth Llechog; a chance to measure your flat out speed!

A kilometre to the west of Porth Wen is Porth Cynfor, called Hell's Mouth by the English (G.R.393949). Whether this is because of the strong gusts emanating from its mouth in a southerly gale, or because of its foaming appearance in a north-easterly gale it is not clear. In any event it is an impressive place, a deep cleft with an entrance so narrow at low water that only a small boat or canoe can beach here. A track lies three hundred steep metres to the south of here.

DINAS GYNFOR

The tidal streams, which are particularly strong around the north coast of Anglesey, attain their maximum rate off the salient points and generally run parallel to the coast. Dinas Gynfor, the northernmost point of Anglesey and the headland to the west of Hell's Mouth, therefore constitutes at least the psychological crux of the trip. On spring tides the stream flows past here at up to five knots (3 knots on neaps), and with an opposing wind or swell this makes for a very choppy sea. The 150 foot high cliffs and sharp barnacled rocks make this an exciting place to be in rough conditions.

Middle Mouse, a small stack lying about a kilometre offshore, affords landing in calm weather. In poor conditions however, it is best avoided. A tide rip runs off Middle Mouse on springs, and the proper name for this islet, Ynys Badrig, stems from the legend that St.Patrick was storm wrecked here after returning from the conversion of Ireland.

Porth Llanlleiana (G.R.387950), the cove west of Dinas Gynfor, affords shelter in offshore winds and a landing place, for the canoeist, in all weathers. The buildings and chimney of a ruined boot factory, and the remains of a quay, are at the head of the cove.

CEMAES

The shore between here and Camaes is full of rocky interest, a more sheltered interlude after the headland. Access and egress at Cemaes is best in Porth Mawr, a large cove in the south eastern corner of the bay. Wylfa power station is conspicuous in the distance on the other side of the bay. Inside Porth Mawr is Cemaes Harbour, with a carpark directly on to the neighbouring beach.

Here is a trip full of character and interest. Taken in the middle hours of the tide it can be very quick, but the rocky coves encourage exploration, and it would be easy to spend half a day along the north coast. And when you have paddled one way, go the other, for on this shore, anticipation is never dulled by experience.

Anglesey East Coast

Access: Moelfre (G.R.513863)
Egress: Lynas Cove (G.R.477929)
Distance: 9 kilometres
Max.Rate of Tidal Streams: 6 knots (springs), 3 knots (neaps)
Tide Races and Overfalls: Point Lynas: Ynys Dulas.
Slack Water Constant: -0.30 (Dulas Bay, North Shore:
H.W.S.-3.30)
Duration of Slack: 0.30

Introduction

The east coast of Anglesey is littered with wrecks, ancient and modern. Past this shore lay the nineteenth century trade route from the eastern empire into Liverpool. North-easterly gales drove many sailing ships, bare masted, their anchors hopelessly dragging, onto this shore. Just ten minutes walk from Moelfre, four hundred and fifty two men, women, and children died from the Royal Charter, Liverpool bound in October 1859. It is the most infamous wreck on the North Wales coast. Many unprintable stories about it abound in the local pubs, and divers are still looking for the ship's gold to this day.

Even in the days of steam however, 'north-easters' can take a heavy toll. Exactly one hundred years to the month after the Royal Charter gale, the six hundred and fifty ton Hindlea was wrecked on this coastline, earning the Moelfre Lifeboat's coxswain his second R.N.L.I. gold medal for gallantry.

Fortunately for the canoeist, where shelter is at a premium, smallness is a virtue, and along this shore there are few bays and inlets where the paddler cannot land. Only off Point Lynas is any great degree of commitment required, and here it can get very rough indeed. It is usually possible however, to sneak past the overfalls close round the headland between Pilot Cove and Lynas Cove.

MOELFRE

Access to the sea at Moelfre is simple enough, being at the harbour slipway from the main A5108. The famous lifeboat station is passed immediately on the left (two bright orange lights at night, visible from the south), and the shore leading out of the harbour is not without interest for rock slalomists. Y Swint, the channel between Ynys Moelfre (sometimes called Rat Island) and the headland, has a small tide rip through it, and dries out at Low Water springs. A light is

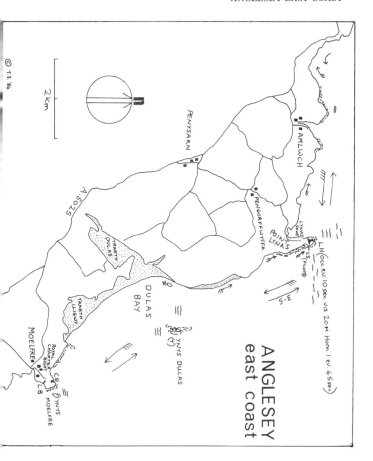

exhibited from a white metal post on the headland (Gp Fl 3 ev 9 sec, Vis 6 M), and an auxiliary manned coastguard lookout stands nearby. Round the corner, just inside Dulas Bay, is Royal Charter Bight, the site of the aforementioned wreck.

DULAS BAY
Once through Y Swint it is best to head straight for Ynys Dulas when going with the ebb stream. If you are paddling against the last of the

125

flood, use may be made of the inshore eddy stream set up in Dulas Bay by the strong offset from Port Lynas. For the last three hours of the flood, the inshore stream sets northward, if only weakly; so, for nine hours out of the twelve, there is a north going stream close inshore along the east coast of Anglesey for up to four kilometres south of Point Lynas.

Ynys Dulas, or Seal Island, offers good landfall for canoeists, and, as the English name suggests, a chance to see seals. There is a slender white tower in the centre of the island, built, like Rhoscolyn beacon, as a landmark and refuge for seamen. There are shelves of rock to the north and south, which, when covered, cause rough water. There are also small overfalls to the west of Ynys Dulas, where a shelf of rock, some four metres beneath the sea, joins the island to the mainland.

In the crook of Dulas Bay is Traeth Dulas, a large area of sand which dries out after half ebb. Small yachts and dinghies sometimes shelter or tie up here, but it is the narrow entrance, called Ceg-y-Trai, which will be of most interest to canoeists. Being only fifteen yards wide, the tide rips through at a fair old rate, particularly on the ebb (up to 6 knots on springs). It should be noted that the flood stream does not enter Traeth Dulas until three hours after high water in the area.

POINT LYNAS

The flood stream tends to be stronger than the ebb along the east coast of Anglesey, and certainly off Point Lynas, the biggest waves are to be found on the east-going stream. On both flood and ebb however, there is a big tide race with overfalls up to a kilometre off Point Lynas. The flood stream sets to the south-east at a maximum rate of 6 knots, while the ebb sets to the north at a maximum rate of 5 knots.

Both flood and ebb tides produce local eddies round Point Lynas. The flood sets up a strong north going stream close inshore to the east side of the headland, while the ebb produces a weaker and shorter eddy stream running east along the north tip of the headland. Both eddy streams offer the more adventurous canoeist a return ride to the meatier water off the headland.

The lighthouse on the headland (Occ W ev. 10 sec, Vis 20M, Horn 1 ev. 45 sec) was built in 1814, and is very similar to the one on the Great Ormes Head. Point Lynas however, will not go out of commission in the foreseeable future, being a key light on the route into Liverpool, and locally of increased importance since the advent of the offshore oil terminal at Amlwch.

On the east side of Point Lynas is Pilot Cove, with the pilot station jetty, from where launches take pilots to and from ships entering and leaving Liverpool Bay. In the eighteenth century, the station was in Lynas Cove, and six oared gigs were used to ferry pilots out to the square riggers. Two fixed red lights are displayed on the jetty when the station is in operation.

The coastline from Traeth Dulas to Point Lynas becomes progressively higher and there is no road access. Once round the headland however, Lynas Cove, otherwise known as Porth Eilean or Llaneilian Cove, offers a small beach leading to a road close to the shore. Those requiring a further work-out can continue to Amlwch, but this tiny beach seems a fitting ending to this deserted, and in some weathers, desolate coastline.

*The old Ten Feet Bank Buoy north-west of Puffin Island -
a new square buoy has recently replaced it. Photo: Derek Mayes*

Puffin Island

Access and Egress: Trwyn Du (G.R.640813)
Distance: c. 5 kilometres
Maximum Rate of Tidal Streams: 3½ knots (springs), 2 knots (neaps)
Overfalls and Tide Races: None of significance
Slack Water Constant: H.W. +0.30, L.W. -0.40
Duration of Slack: 0.30

Introduction

The easternmost point of Anglesey is marked by a precipitous mass of rock nearly a mile long, four hundred yards wide, and two hundred feet high. It is an island of great character in an outstanding situation. It is sufficiently easy of access to provide a dramatic and exciting trip for diblers and dablers in the sport of sea canoeing. It is also one of the best places in North Wales to see nesting sea birds.

Puffin Island or Ynys Seiriol, also called Priestholm, is most easily approached by way of Beaumaris, thereafter keeping to the south-east coast road until it ends near Penmon Priory. Here a toll must be paid (in summer) to gain admittance to the headland of Trwyn-du. A café and coastguard station are open on summer weekends, and a shingle beach offers easy access to the sea.

PUFFIN STRAIT

The strait between Trwyn-du and Puffin Island is marked by a lighthouse and beacon. The black and white banded lighthouse automatic (Fl W ev 5½s, vis 15m, Bell) and the perpetual tolling of its bell together with the boldly printed message 'no passage landward', stirs the imagination to thoughts of shipwreck and storm. The red and white conical beacon is much smaller and less conspicuous (no light) than the lighthouse. It is equally crucial for large boats however, in that it marks the south-western extremity of Puffin Island and the north side of this north-western entrance to the Menai Strait. Canoeists, beware the trawler skipper drowsing after a long session in the wheelhouse.

The Tides

In the middle two hours of the tide, the stream can run through the strait at nearly four knots, so a fairly radical ferry glide may be necessary to cross from the lighthouse to the eddies off the island. Round the island itself, the tides are less strong and it is easy to paddle against them. This may well be necessary on one side or the other. The ebb tide runs from south-west to north-east up the south-east

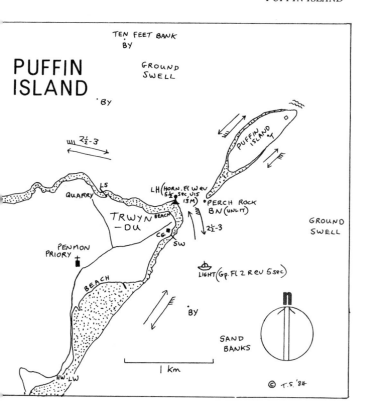

shore, and the flood runs from north-east to south-west down the
north-west shore, while at both ends of the island the ebb runs west
and the flood east. At the northern tip of the island, a small tide race
develops in the middle hours of the tide, particularly noticeable on the
ebb. This is easily avoided by a passage close in-shore. Seals are often
seen here, being particularly friendly in June and July.

PUFFIN ISLAND

The cliffs and caves of the island are most dramatic on the north west
shore. This is usually the lee shore and with a 'nor-wester' blowing the
long fetch to Ireland makes for a rough sea. Seething waves, foaming

129

and frothing their fettered disgust in the caverns of Puffin, combined
with the cries of cormorants and shags, guillemots and razorbills,
kittiwakes and fulmars, to produce a wild beauty here. Even a pair of
peregrine falcons found this place inhospitable enough to nest a few
years back.

A steep path leads to the summit of this bird sanctuary from the
south-west tip of the island. Unfortunately all but half a dozen Puffin
have disappeared, their burrows infested by egg stealing rats, escaped
no doubt, from some sinking ship. There is however, the tower to see.
Built by the hermit Saint Seirol on the highest point of land, it serves
as an important reference point for sailors. The other building, less
visible on the north-east end of the Puffin Island, is the old Semaphore
Telegraph Station built in 1811. This was part of a chain of Telegraph
posts stretching from Holy Mountain to Liverpool, capable in good
visibility, of passing and receiving a message in thirty seconds.

TRWYN DINMOOR

To the west of Puffin is a large red and white spherical buoy, Ten Feet
Bank Buoy (no light). A visit to this, and then to the Dinmoor quarry
jetties, due south on the Anglesey shore (G.R.633815), makes an
interesting extension to the trip. The headland west of the quarries
Trwyn Dinmoor (G.R.630817), is also well worth a visit, even as a trip
by itself, if a strong offshore wind makes a circumnavigation imprac-
ticable. Whatever the decision you will soon be back. A cry on the
breeze, a curl of breaking water, a touch of history, the feel of
isolation, an unforgettable place to be.

Trwyn-du lighthouse - Puffin Island. Photo: Derek Mayes

The Menai Strait

Access: Menai Bridge (G.R.565716)
Egress: Nelson's Jetty (G.R.530709); or Port Dinorwic
(G.R.521674); or Caernarfon (G.R.477625)
Distance: 3 kilometres; or 7 kilometres; or 14 kilometres
Max. Rate of Tidal Streams: 8 knots
Tide Race and Overfalls: The Swellies
Slack Water Constant: Menai Bridge -2.00; Caernarfon -1.15
Duration of Slack: (springs) 0.15; (neaps) 0.30

Introduction

The Menai Strait separates the island of Anglesey from the mainland
of North Wales. Between Caernarfon and Port Dinorwic
(G.R.526678), a distance of seven kilometres, the Strait is very like a
river estuary, broad, silted with sand, and the site of many yacht
anchorages. Between Port Dinorwic and Menai Bridge, a further
seven kilometres, the Strait becomes narrow and rocky, winding its
way between steep sides assuming something of the character of a
river canyon. At its narrowest point the Strait is crossed by two
bridges, Telford's Suspension Bridge to the east and Stephenson's
Britannia Tubular Bridge to the west.

The area between the two bridges is known locally as The Swellies.
It is a popular place for canoeists practicing white water techniques
with powerful jets between the bridge supports, and rough water
round the various small islands. As a whole, the Menai Strait offers
fast water in a relatively safe, because confined, environment. A useful
place when the rivers are dry, or when the wind is too strong out to
sea, but also a fascinating trip in its own right.

Tidal Streams

The tidal streams in the Menai Strait are swift and strong in both
directions. On the strength of the spring tide the water surges through
the Swellies at seven or eight knots, a rate only exceeded at two other
points on Britain's coastline, the Alderney race and the Pentland
Firth. Between Port Dinorwic and Caernarfon the stream slackens off
to a mere five knots! It is possible to paddle against the tide in the
Strait by using the eddies close inshore; possible, but extremely
tedious and time consuming. Accurate prediction of the tidal streams,
therefore, is the key, not only to catching the most exciting white
water, but also simply to an enjoyable and relaxing paddle through the
Strait.

Such a prediction is not easy. High and Low water at Menai Bridge

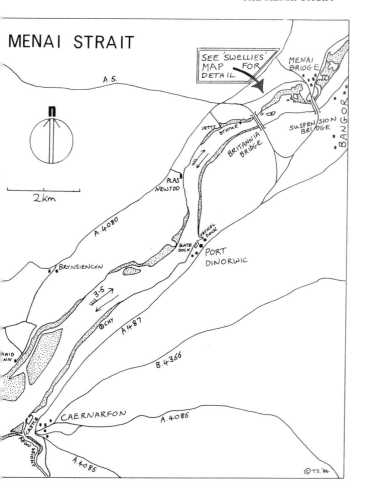

oes not coincide with Slack Water, and there is an appreciable
ifference between the times of High and Low water at Caernarfon
nd Menai Bridge. A close look at the tidal peculiarities of the Strait
, therefore, necessary before proceeding to a general description of
e trip.

High and Low Water

High and Low water at Caernarfon occurs at approximately the same time as Slack Water, which is one and a quarter hours before Liverpool. Fourteen kilometres further north in the Swellies, High and Low water occur about *forty-five* minutes later. One would expect the difference here to be about *thirty* minutes, since that between Llandwyn Island and Puffin Island, thirty kilometres apart at either end of the Strait, is only an hour. This anomaly is caused by the fact that the tidal streams meet and diverge close to the Swellies, tending to retard the times of High and Low water.

Slack Water

This confluence and separation of tidal streams, which takes place N.E. of the Swellies, just S.W. of Beaumaris, accounts for a further and crucial anomaly. *Slack Water in the Swellies occurs about an hour and a half before High and Low Water in the area*, or about two hours before High and Low Water at Liverpool. So while the time of High and Low Water is retarded, the time of Slack Water is advanced. To understand why this happens, a description of the tidal flow helps.

The Flood

The young flood coming up from Caernarfon meets little or no opposition as it proceeds towards the N.E. end of the Strait, for there, it is still ebbing round the north coast. The level of the tide in the Swellies, in fact, decreases for about an hour and a half while the stream flows in a N.E. direction.

As the flood starts to come in at the N.E. end, so the tide begins to rise again. The flood at the N.E. end eventually dominates the weakening flood at the S.W. end, so that the ebb stream starts flowing in the Swellies about three quarters of an hour before it does in Caernarfon, and the water level continues to rise for a further three-quarters of an hour. Thus the stream in the Swellies turns to the S.W. about an hour and a half before High Water is reached.

The Ebb

At Puffin Island the rise of the tide above chart datum is higher (by about three metres) than at Caernarfon. Because more water pools in Liverpool Bay than Caernarfon Bay, the ebb is stronger, and runs quicker for longer, than the flood. So the best white water sport in the Swellies may be had in the middle three hours of the flood and the middle four hours of the ebb.

About two hours before Low Water at Liverpool the tide begins to ebb E. past Beaumaris, and the S.W. stream in the Swellies grinds to a halt. However the water level continues to drop for a further hour and a half.

MENAI BRIDGE

Slack Water on both ebb and flood lasts for a very short time in the Swellies - fifteen minutes on springs and thirty minutes on neaps. To see the water almost screech to a halt and then rev up and go the other way, is a sight well worth waiting for. The best place to view this aquatic rallycross is, logically, at the narrowest part of the Strait, Menai Bridge, and this also offers a convenient point of departure for the trip described here - it goes, almost without saying, that a trip from Caernarfon or Port Dinorwic on the flood, is equally plausible.

A small road leading from the roundabout on the Anglesey side of the Suspension Bridge leads to an even smaller parking place under the bridge supports. A strong eddy forms behind the north bridge support, and there are smaller, but no less strong eddies, behind the other bridge supports on the northern side of the Strait. These eddies, and the fast moving water between, are excellent for practising white water techniques.

THE SWELLIES

The rocks and islets between Telford's Suspension Bridge and Stephenson's Britannia Tubular Bridge also provide good sport in the middle hours of the tide. An enormous standing wave forms over Swelly Rock on the flood, breaking into a stopper wave every now and then. At Gored Goch, a small island with a whitewashed cottage, stone tower and flagstaff, the stream runs strongly on either side. On the flood there is a bedrock rapid on the southern side, while on the ebb there is a good little standing wave on the northern side. Close to the south side of the island are some old fish traps with iron spikes providing a hazard to canoeists. Finally, further west the stream divides strongly round Britannia Rock, which supports the central pier of that bridge, forming strong eddies on the downstream side.

PORT DINORWIC

The Strait between Britannia Bridge and Port Dinorwic makes a broad sweep to the left between the wooden slopes of Vaynol Park on the mainland and Plas Newydd on the Anglesey shore. Between Britannia Bridge and the spectacular country house of Plas Newydd, there is a good egress point for those wanting a short trip. It is a stone jetty (accessible from the A.4080 just after turning off the A.5) seven hundred metres west of the Statue of Nelson, the latter all the more

135

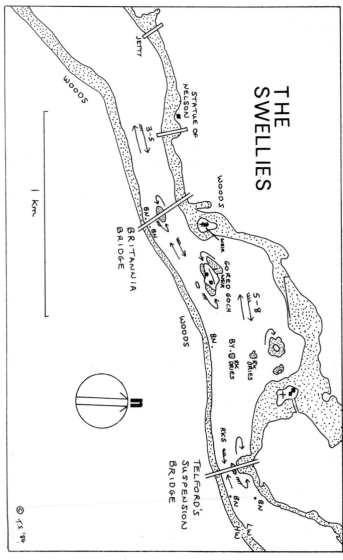

THE SWELLIES

visible for the depredations of countless seagulls.

Port Dinorwic, lying about four kilometres south-west of Britannia Bridge on the mainland shore, and the site of many yacht anchorages, offers another chance to shorten the trip. Vaynol Dock is passed first, with its lock gates, followed by the old open slate dock. Finally there is the landing jetty, above which a small cafe offers welcome refreshment. A road passes between the houses and the shore at this point.

CAERNARFON

The Strait to the south-west of Port Dinorwic gradually broadens out to twice its width. Although the speed of the tidal stream slackens correspondingly, the remainder of the trip may be enlivened by the action of the wind in this less sheltered waterway. If the wind is against the tide, as the prevailing wind tends to be on the ebb, quite a chop can be stirred up. If on the other hand, you are starting from Caernarfon and the wind is with you, the rate and duration of the flood may be substantially increased.

The town of Caernarfon is situated, on the southern side of the Strait and on the right bank of the estuary of the River Seiont - so it would be possible to go from Llanberis to Beaumaris without leaving your canoe! Prominent from the Strait is the castle built by Edward I, under whose walls there is now a convenient car park. To reach your transport, paddle under the swing bridge, into the Seiont, and pull out under the slate quay which runs for six hundred metres along the right bank of the river. Unfortunately running this trip on the ebb means floundering across mud at the end.

Disillusionment with the extent of your fatigue, or surprised pleasure at the speed of your passage, are equally possible emotions at the end of this trip. And it will depend as much on your planning, as on your strength. For the Menai Strait will test the judgement of the most experienced sea canoeist, with its tidal gradient, tidal differences, and powerful streams. This is certainly an outstanding voyage for anyone interested in tidal planning. And there is the added attraction of white water in the Swellies and beautiful scenery throughout.

The Ormes

Access: Llandudno West Shore (G.R.763825)
Egress: Llandudno North Shore (G.R.7982)
Distance: 10 kilometres
Max. Rate of Tidal Streams: 3 knots (springs), 2 knots (neaps)
Tide Race: Great Ormes Head
Slack Water Constant: -0.24
Duration of Slack: 0.30

Introduction

From the sea, Great Ormes Head is one of the best landmarks on the north coast of Wales. The north face of the promontory is a sheer limestone cliff over four hundred feet in height, stretching for three kilometres on an east-west axis. Two miles east is Little Ormes Head, little only by comparison, and actually higher as an unbroken cliff. Although the trip round these headlands is serious because of the lack of egress, the tidal planning is straightforward and the streams relatively weak. One does not have to be an expert therefore, to seize the chance of a glide past the limestone heights.

GREAT ORME

The trip may be done very well in either direction. As described here the Great Orme is visited first so the paddler will want to use the flood. The best access point is Llandudno West Shore, gained from the road alongside. Two kilometres of relatively sheltered paddling, takes the canoeist to Hornby Cave, a dramatic sanctuary for sea life of all kinds. The north-west extremity of Great Orme is marked by a lighthouse, a white square castellated stone tower standing 300 feet above the sea. This is going out of commission as I write, in March 1985.

During the spring tides the stream sets strongly off the north-west point of Great Orme setting up a tide race. In opposing winds the waves can get big here, and in any swell there is clapotis off the cliffs up to one hundred metres offshore. In calm conditions it is possible to paddle against the tide keeping close in to the cliffs, and using the eddies there.

LLANDUDNO BAY

Once round the headland, the lookout at Pen-trwyn comes into view, and below is Pigeon Cave, which, at Low Water, provides a dramatic lunch spot (there is a way out of this cave, to the cliffs above, through some exciting holes, although no canoe could go this way). Further round still, and Llandudno pier comes into sight (light exhibited at

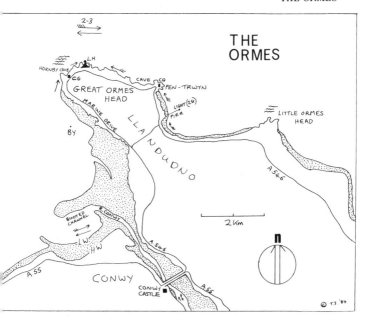

night). Tidal streams in Llandudno Bay are negligible, so, even if the tide has turned, it is a relatively simple matter to paddle across it to Little Orme. Here the canoeist can watch the antics of guillemots, razorbills, puffins, and, an even rarer breed, in contemporary Britain, the aid climber. Egress may be made anywhere along Llandudno North Shore, the pebble beach which stretches for two and half kilometres between Llandudno pier and Little Orme.

The proximity of street lights at access and egress makes this paddle relatively easy at night. A further ingredient makes the dark trip popular. The phosphorus widely distributed along this coastline gives a luminous glow at night, as it undergoes slow combustion. Dancing lights on your bow wave, jagged moon shadows, and the rolling chorus of breaking waves, an eerie experience, an unforgettable night.

Out through the surf.   Photo: Derek Mayes

THE
SURF GUIDE

Coastal Surf

Introduction

The indented coastline of North Wales can provide excellent surf. Only two beaches however, Hell's Mouth and Porth Ceiriad, can compare with 'Surf City U.K.' - the north coast of Cornwall. Off North Wales, these are the only beaches which receive an uninterrupted swell from the Atlantic. Surfable waves coming out of a glassy sea - the surfers dream - are almost unknown elsewhere along the coast.

It may be necessary to make the long drive down the Lleyn Peninsula to find swell generated surf, but good wind generated surf can be found on Anglesey. And because it is an island, Anglesey usually has a beach facing the wind somewhere along its coast.

Predicting *when* there will be surf is notoriously difficult. Swell hitting North Wales from the Atlantic is usually associated with approaching depressions, particularly when there is a steep pressure gradient between the centre of the depression and Wales. For wind generated surf, the strength of the wind on the day is much less important than the strength of it over the previous forty-eight hours. Indeed a strong onshore wind tends to flatten the waves, and makes the paddle out beyond the break even more difficult.

Knowing *where* the surf will be is not easy either. Britain's prevailing winds come from the south-west, so naturally it is beaches facing that direction which usually have the surf. I have already mentioned Hell's Mouth and Porth Ceiriad on the Lleyn; on Anglesey, Cable Bay and Rhosneigr are the most popular.

Wind generated surf however, can come from any direction. Again the direction of the wind on the day is less important than the direction in which it has been blowing for the previous forty-eight hours. That will determine where the waves are coming from, and a last minute offshore wind may peak the waves nicely for surfing.

Almost all the surfable 'breaks' in North Wales are 'beach breaks'. The waves travel up a gradually shelving beach and break as they reach shallower water. It follows that wherever the beach slopes less (Low Water) the surf will tend to flatten out, and wherever the beach steepens (High Water) the surf will tend to dump. This is why surf tends to be best from mid to high tide - the waves are running where the beach shelves at the 'right' angle. Surf is often better on the flood than on the ebb, because the waves are being pushed in by the rising tide.

All surf beaches have rips, some large, some small. These are

141

currents of water going out to sea. Viewed at Low Water, a gully will usually show where the rip runs, and, at high tide, an area of darker water may indicate where this is. Rips are useful to the canoeist, but dangerous for the swimmer. Those caught in one should head across the current parallel with the beach; once in the surf again, the swimmer will be carried back into the beach.

The other main dangers in surfing are collisions - with rocks, other canoeists, and swimmers. Fortunately, most beaches mentioned here are, except at the sides, rock free, but a look at low tide will reveal any areas to avoid. The effects of a collision with another canoeist can be dramatically reduced by capsizing before impact (thus slowing the boat), and not surfing in slalom boats with pointed spear-like ends. Finally, it is common sense not to surf where there are people swimming.

Listed below are the best surf beaches on the North Wales coast. A Grid Reference identifies their position on the appropriate 1:50,000 Ordnance Survey Map, and the numbers refer to marked locations on the Flood Stream Tidal map in this Guide. It may only be possible to shoot the tube, or lip turn the curl, on a few days, and at a few places, - the few will be enough - but, for the rest, there is much fun to be had in short runs, in lining up for pop outs, pirouettes, and pearl dives, in bongoing the soup, even in fighting through a closed out break line. Good surf is hard to find, but good fun is not.

THE SURF BEACHES
Numbers Refer to Marked Locations on Flood Stream Tidal Map.

1. Black Rock Sands (G.R.3753)
This beach is crowded in summer, and the surf is mediocre. However, it is very accessible, and worth trying if you don't fancy the long haul to Anglesey, or along the narrow roads of the Lleyn. Black Rock Sands faces south-west.

2. Porth Ceiriad (G.R.3124)
This superb, secluded, south facing surf beach has the added advantage of a campsite overlooking the bay. Access to this site is by a rough track leading from the farm at Pant-y-branner. The best surf runs into the north-east corner of the bay. It tends to be fast and steep, good therefore for kayaks, but not for skis. There can be surf at Porth Ceiriad when everywhere else is flat.

3. Hell's Mouth (G.R.2428 to G.R.2825)
Hell's Mouth is the *best* surf beach in North Wales. It faces south-west. There will be plenty of boards here when the surf is running.

The best break is in the south-eastern corner; when it is too big there, the north-western corner provides a refuge. Roads lead to both ends, but some cunning and an Ordnance Survey Map is needed to find the closest approach to the former.

4. Aberdaron (G.R.172263)

This pleasant south-facing sandy beach fronts a picturesque village, which is the usual departure point for the classic Bardsey crossing. The waves are smallest opposite the slipway, and increase in size as you go eastwards along the beach. At high water the waves can dump quite badly.

5. Dinas Dinlle (G.R.4356 to G.R.4358)

A west south-west facing beach with gently shelving sand at Low Water and a steep shingle bank at High Water. The latter causes the waves to dump. The best surf is at mid-tide.

6. Newborough Warren (G.R.3863 to G.R.4261)

Unfortunately, the south-west facing picturesque beach at Newborough is not well shaped for surf. It is, however, a safe beach for beginners. Surf is most often found to the west of Llanddwyn Island, so a trip round this beautiful and unspoilt headland can be added to the day out. (See description in this Guide)

7. Cable Bay (Porth Trecastell) (G.R.332706)

An excellent narrow fan-shaped cove which peaks the waves beautifully on occasions. This west facing bay is very popular with surfers, and second only in quality to Hell's Mouth. There are two strong rip currents, one on either side of the bay. The southerly rip running along the cliffs to the left as you look out to sea, is very strong. A well preserved chambered burial mound lies on the cliff to the north, the last resting place, no doubt, for prehistoric surfers. If there is no surf here, check Rhosneigr, two kilometres to the north.

8. Rhosneigr (G.R.3271)

This beach faces south-west and sometimes has good surf when Cable Bay is poor. It is quite popular, despite a number of rocky outcrops. The surf increases in size towards the north. The Afon Crigyll creates a rip. Much used by windsurfers.

9. Trearddur Bay (G.R.2578)

A west south-west facing beach which can be good when Cable Bay, and Rhosneigr are blown out. Also popular with windsurfers.

10. Sandy Beach (G.R.2885)

The best beach after a north-westerly wind. There is a good campsite right next to the sand.

11. Bull Bay (G.R.4294)
A north facing beach which can produce some fair surf. Rocks tend to get in the way at high tide.

12. Traeth Lligwy (G.R.4987)
This beach faces east, and it is one of the few places where you may get some sport when windy anti-cyclonic conditions prevail.

Tidal Bores

Introduction
A tidal bore is a wave moving up the lower reaches of a river, sometimes good, occasionally ideal, for surfing. Conditions for a bore are a wide estuary converging into a narrow river mouth, a rising river bed, and a large tide. The size of the bore will be affected by the prevailing wind direction, the strength of the wind, and by the freshwater level in the river. With so many variables, it is not surprising that tidal bores are notoriously hard to predict.

There are two bores along the Welsh coast which are of interest to the canoeist, and although strictly speaking they lie outside the area of this Guide, they are popular with both locals and visitors. The Severn Bore is further from North Wales (150 miles from Capel Curig), but is larger than the Dee Bore.

Bores can be dangerous. They will carry floating objects a long way - one local *habitué* surfed beside a 50 gallon drum for five hundred yards. They are hard to pick up, and hard to get off. They pass through bridge pillars, under trees, along rugged banks, between moored boats, around stanchions, and over weirs. So don't take 'the ultimate ride' too literally.

THE SEVERN BORE
Any tide over 7.9 metres at Sharpness will create a bore on the Severn. Larger tides, combined with a strong south-westerly wind and a high freshwater level (but not *too* high), will create a spectacular bore, with a wave of up to 6 feet.

A good place for kayaks to pick up the Bore is Newnham on the A.48 south-west of Gloucester. Weak paddlers are advised to get off the river by Westbury. After this the wave steepens, becoming suitable for skis and shoes. Strong paddlers can continue as far as Minsterworth, or even Gloucester Weir (get off before the Weir). Rea Strait (G.R.810164) is probably the most popular start for skis.

The time of high water at Sharpness coincides approximately with the time that the Bore reaches Minsterworth. The Bore at Stonebench is 10 minutes later, and at Over Bridge 35 minutes later. The times for the Bore in the upper estuary are, Epney 20 minutes *before* Minsterworth, Newnham 60 minutes before, and Fretherne 85 minutes before. Allow plenty of time for crowded roads.

THE DEE BORE

Any tide over 9 metres at Liverpool will produce a bore on the Dee. Larger tides, combined with strong north-westerly winds and a high freshwater level (again, *too* high, and the bore is overwhelmed), produces a large bore, up to 3 feet high.

The Dee Bore runs from Queensferry to Chester Weir. The best place to put in, is Saltney Ferry on the south shore. From here, paddle downstream until 500 metres above the road (A.550) bridge at Queensferry. Here the wave can be picked up - *under* the bridge, the wave *decreases* in height - for the ride back upstream.

The bore passes Queensferry bridge between 2 and 1½ hours before high water at Liverpool. It is often difficult to keep on the wave as it passes a sharp bend the Chester side of Saltney Ferry.

APPENDICES

Appendix I
THE SEA BIRDS OF NORTH WALES
By Nigel Foster

All year round, in the shelter of the Menai Straits, the haunting flute-like call of the curlew and the shrill cry of the black and white oystercatcher can be heard, and the hunched and stiff figure of the heron can be seen, like an old grey man at the waters edge. But it is springtime that sees the arrival of thousands of sea birds to North Wales, a touch of magic to the area that lasts until summer is nearly over.

For me the arrival of the puffins to join the already massive flocks of whirring auks, and the arrival of the terns soon afterwards, with their twisting dive and distinctive cries, are the two landmarks I most eagerly await.

The kayak presents a unique opportunity to observe sea birds at close range without alarming them. Puffins in particular are often so unbothered by the approach of a kayak, that they will sit and watch, until it is almost touching them, before they dive or flap a few yards across the water. However, it is possible to cause great loss of nests, eggs and chicks by careless movement close to nesting cliffs, or by landing and walking around. With a little observation it is easy to see when the birds are starting to get uneasy or alarmed. A gentle paddle out to sea will then preserve the peace, and safeguard the birds.

AUKS
The auks can be likened to the penguins of the southern hemisphere. They sit upright like penguins and have black and white or dark brown and white plumage.

Puffins are probably the best known and liked of this group. They are noted for their brilliantly coloured beak. At a distance the beak, together with the large white circle around each eye that covers almost the whole side of the head, makes the puffin easy to spot amongst flocks of other auks. Puffins are unbelievably clumsy on land. I have seen puffins land on their beaks on front of their nesting burrows, do belly flops and even somersaults whilst trying to land. When the puffin has hatched its egg, it can be seen carrying beakfuls of sand eels, each silvery fish held neatly in a row with its head and tail sticking out on either side of the beak.

The razorbill and guillemot are two common species of auk in this area. The razorbill has a large thick beak and black and white plumage whereas the guillemot has a finer, more cylindrical beak which helps to emphasize a more streamlined profile. The plumage is dark brown and white. As the flocks of birds whirr overhead with rapid wingbeats it is easy to spot the difference in colour and profile.

The guillemot nests in large colonies on steep cliffs, in row upon row of smart birds, whereas the razorbills often prefer to nest in less precipitous surroundings, hiding beneath boulders or choosing less extensive ledges.

There is a fourth species of auk to be seen in North Wales, the **black guillemot,** although it is not widespread or numerous. Predominantly a more northern bird, the black plumage with a conspicuous white spot on the wing is unmistakable for anything else. It is slightly smaller than the razorbill and guillemot, being more the size of a puffin. In flight the flash of the white wing spot, and the red legs and feet which are often trailed behind to aid steering, make identification of this attractive bird easy.

TERNS
In North Wales we are lucky to have five nesting species of tern, the sandwich, arctic, common, roseate, and little tern. The first three are the more numerous, the larger sandwich tern with its harsh grating call 'karrick', its short legs and ruffled plumage at the back of its head, the arctic tern with its more musical yet piercing 'kee-yar', and the common tern, almost identical to the arctic tern until viewed closely, when the beak appears slightly shorter owing to a black tip to an otherwise similar red beak. The call of the common tern is a long harsh 'kree-ee'.

Terns nest in colonies on the ground and vigorously protect the colony from predators by flying out in large numbers to dive bomb them. They have narrow graceful wings and often have tail streamers. In flight the beak is inclined downwards, unlike that of the gull which is pointed forwards.

Groups of terns fishing present a fascinating spectacle, calling loudly and suddenly folding their wings close to the body and plunging almost vertically in a twisting dive into the water. Most of these dives are from a height of at least fifteen feet and almost all end in the capture of a small fish.

GULLS
The larger gulls are present all the year round. **The herring gull** must be the worst of the scavengers, ranging inland to pester the tourists on the summit of Snowdon in search of a meal. There are two varieties of black backed gull. The **greater black backed gull** is a massive

predatory bird with jet black back, pink legs and an appetite for puffins, shear-waters, chicks and eggs. Less numerous than herring gulls, there are always a handful of these birds to be seen cruising around the nesting cliffs. They in turn nest on the ground on the flatter grassy tops of islands and cliffs. The **lesser black backed gull** is about the size of a herring gull, but has a darker grey back and yellow legs, unlike the pink legs of the other two birds.

The **kittiwake** is a smaller gull, more dove-like in appearance with an onomatopoeic call that makes its presence noticeable often before the bird is spotted. Nests are cemented on tiny ledges on the steepest cliffs, often around cave entrances. When the adult bird is sitting, the tail and their black wing tips jut out of the nest, so that the cliff below becomes streaked with white bird lime. The beak is a greenish yellow and lacks the hook and the red spot of the beaks of the previous mentioned gulls.

The **common gull** and **black headed gull** are less commonly seen.

The **gannet** is only occasionally seen around North Wales. Much more common are two related, although different looking, gulls, the **cormorant and shag.** By drifting gently downtide past the boulders at the bottom of cliffs it is possible to pass shags at a distance of ten feet without them taking flight. The greenish sheen to the dark plumage, the bright yellow base of the beak and the tuft of feathers on the head distinguish the shag from its larger relative the cormorant, which in the spring has a prominent white spot behind the wing. The shag usually nests close to the water often in hollows beneath boulders, whereas the cormorant favours a higher nesting place on the top of cliffs or on high rocky outcrops. Both birds dive for fish, and as the plumage becomes waterlogged, the bird will gradually sink until only the snake-like neck and head extends from the water. Both birds stand with wings outstretched to dry the plumage after fishing.

A less endearing habit of the shag is to raise its tail, hunch its body and forcibly eject a jet of excrement in preparation for take-off. When experienced at close quarters this can prove to be most unpleasant. Take off itself is fairly hit and miss, with the bird flapping its untidy wings frantically as it ascends, often not gaining enough lift to prevent a crash into the water. On a calm day, however, their graceful flight underwater can be watched, revealing where their true skill lies.

PETRELS

The petrels are an interesting group of birds. They are related to the albatross and are true ocean goers. The one that we see most frequently is the **fulmar**, and surprisingly this is the one that started nesting in this area only relatively recently, when the fulmar rapidly extended its range southwards to include almost all of the British coast. The fulmar is a pale bird with grey back and yellow beak; similar in appearance to a gull, but easily distinguished by its stiff winged flight; rather like a gull with arthritis. The beak, like that of all the petrels, has two external nostrils which appear as tubes that lie on the top of the beak. This gives a stepped profile to the beak that is quite easy to spot. The fulmar also has a patch of dark feathers around a dark eye. In remote areas the fulmar will nest almost anywhere, from grassy walls, on open ground, rabbit holes or vegetated cliff ledges. Fulmars pay kayak paddlers more attention than most birds do. On open water a fulmar will often change its course to circle closely, almost brushing the water with its wing tip as it scrutinises the kayak with a dark eye.

The commonly known nest defence of the fulmar is its ability to produce an evil smelling oil, which it spits out when approached too closely. Many sea birds will regurgitate food when alarmed; a habit taken advantage of by kleptoparasitic birds like the skuas. The appearance of this revolting oil must come as a bit of a disappointment to attacking birds. Once smelled, the scent is always recognised, so that the presence of a colony of fulmars can be detected by scent.

The other petrels nesting in North Wales, the **shearwater** and the **storm petrel,** are both preyed on extensively by birds such as the black backed gulls. For this reason they only approach land by night, and are perhaps less well known because of this. Seen floating together in great rafts offshore, the Manx shearwaters appear to be predominantly black, but when seen in flight, scything effortlessly across the waves at high speed, the white undersides become a characteristic feature, and the birds appear to change colour from black to white as they turn to expose their undersides.

The tiny storm petrel is no bigger than a swallow. On a rough day takes a sharp eye to spot the tiny dark shape hurrying across the waves, so it is suprising to learn that storm petrels are among the commonest sea birds. In the St. Kilda islands they were nicknamed the 'ferrymen' because of their nocturnal habit of flying backwards and forwards along a stretch of dry stone wall in the attempt to identify the quiet churring of their partner on the nest.

OTHER SPECIES

Amongst the less common sea cliff dwellers in North Wales are the **red billed chough,** appearing rather like a crow until its fine red bill and red legs become visible or its distinctive call is recognised, and the

peregrine falcon.

There are many other species of bird to be seen around the North Wales coast, and many of the waders and ducks can be approached fairly closely by kayak. However, it is the sea birds that really stand out so closely from a kayak, that binoculars become superfluous.

SEALS

Anyone who spends time watching sea birds around North Wales, will in turn be subject to a certain amount of scrutiny by seals. These fascinating and inquisitive mammals will often repeatedly approach a patient paddler until curiosity overcomes fear. I have had my kayak examined from end to end, my paddle gently pushed, and my elbow nudged by a female seal. Female Atlantic grey seals have quite a pretty face compared to the conical head of the bulls!

The new Ten Feet Bank Buoy off Puffin Island.
Photo: Derek Mayes

Appendix II

LONG DISTANCE SEA JOURNEYS

It does not fall within the context of this guide to describe long distance trips in any detail. The advanced sea kayaker will have his own sources - only one of which will be this guide - for planning such a journey. So the following are simply offered as suggestions.

THE CIRCUMNAVIGATION OF ANGLESEY

This has developed into something of a race amongst local canoeists. The record, at present, stands at 14 hours, although one local lad did Moelfre to Puffin in 10½ hours - stopping one hour short of an incredible time, because his wife was expecting him home! Do not let these times fool you however; it is about 70 nautical miles around the island, and few can do that sort of distance in one go.

The circumnavigation is most easily accomplished by keeping out to sea in Red Wharf, Holyhead, Penrhos, and Cymran Bays. This reduces the distance, and allows the maximum help to be gained from a favourable tidal stream. Where a choice is unavoidable, use the stream in the Menai Strait, and around the north and west coasts, and paddle against it on the east and south-west coasts. The latter has the weakest tidal streams, so it is relatively easy to fight the tide between Rhosneigr and Llandwyn. A tide of more than 9 metres at Liverpool is probably necessary for the non-stop trip.

THE LLEYN PENINSULA

The full trip, from Bangor to Cricieth, is about the same distance as the circumnavigation of Anglesey (70 nautical miles). It does not, in the same way, encourage a non-stop journey. The tides are less strong over the majority of the way, and there is no Menai Strait to allow the use of both phases of the tide. But, as a two or three day trip, it is well worth considering.

The Lleyn is wilder than Anglesey, particularly on the north coast. This may recommend it to the paddler who wants to get away from it all. The least spoilt is between Trevor and Abersoch. Combined with night on Bardsey, this journey is the naturalist's choice.

ANGLESEY TO THE ISLE OF MAN

This has been done a number of times from Anglesey. I have no information on the reverse crossing. Canoeists have chosen either Cemaes or Bull Bay as their point of departure, and arrived at Ca

Island on the Isle of Man. The crossing is 41 nautical miles.

It seems best to leave about two hours before low water at Holyhead. Tidal assistance is not all that great, as it tends to push you north-east for most of the flood. There are strong tidal streams round Calf Island, so the time of arrival is important. Kemp's 'Cruising Guide to the Isle of Man' is the best authority on local tides. It seems that the Tidal Atlas is misleading in its description of tides here.

HOLYHEAD TO DUBLIN

This Irish Sea crossing has been completed a few times, but it remains a major achievement. The distance is 56 nautical miles. The first crossing was in 1969 (twenty-two hours), and in 1978 it was soloed for the first time, in twenty six hours. Just staying awake in a kayak for that length of time is a major problem.

In terms of tidal assistance, the direction matters little, since the canoeist must cross the tidal streams at right angles (due east or west), the effects cancelling each other out. Perhaps arrival in Dublin has proved the most popular, because of the friendly offlying lighthouses (Bailey and Kish) - and the problems caused by the tide races off Holy Island have been dealt with while fresh.

Appendix III

COASTGUARD AND LIFEBOAT STATIONS

Numbers Relating To Positions on Ebb Stream Map	Town	Coastguard	Lifeboat
1.	Cricieth	None	I.L.B.
2.	Pwllheli	C.S.	S.L.B.
3.	Abersoch	A.W.R.	I.L.B.
4.	Aberdaron	A.W.R.	None
5.	Porth Dinllaen	C.S.	S.L.B.
6.	Llandwrog	A.R.	None
7.	Rhosneigr	A.R.	None
8.	Rhoscolyn	A.W.R.	None
9.	*Holyhead*	*R.H.Q.* (Tel.0407 2051)	S.L.B.
10.	Cemaes	C.S.	None
11.	Moelfre	A.W.R.	S.L.B.
12.	Penmon	C.S.	None
13.	Beaumaris	None	S.L.B. & I.L.B.
14.	Conwy	None	I.L.B.
15.	Llandudno	C.S.	S.L.B. & I.L.B.

The abbreviations used above are used to denote the type of watch kept (Coastguard), and the type of boat stationed (Lifeboat). Their meaning is as follows:

R.H.Q.   District Rescue Headquarters, constantly manned day and night. Telex and emergency telephone services.

C.S.   Coastguard Station, manned for day watch only. Watch extended depending on weather and casualty risk.

A.W.R.   Auxiliary Watch and Rescue Equipment. Auxiliary Coastguard Station sets watch according to weather and casualty risk.

A.R.   Auxiliary Rescue Equipment only. No watch kept.

S.L.B.   Standard (Offshore) Lifeboat.

I.L.B.   Inshore Lifeboat.

Appendix IV
DICTIONARY OF WELSH WORDS
**The meaning of Welsh words, suffixes, and prefixes, used
in the Guidebook, on the Admiralty Charts, and on Ordnance
Survey Maps**

Aber	mouth	Glan	brink, edge
Afon	river	Glass	green/blue
Bach (Fach)	small	Gors	bog
		Gwyn (wyn) m.	white
Blaen	head of valley		
Braich	spur	Gwynt	wind
Bren, Bron	breast of hill	Hafod	summer dwelling
Bryn	hill	Hendre	old
Brynog	rushes or rushy	Isaf	lower
Bwlch	pass, saddle	Llan	clearing, Church
Cafr	fort	Llwybr	footpath
Canol	middle	Llyn	lake
Capel	Chapel, Church	Maen	stone
Carnedd	cairn	Maes, Cae	field
Carreg/ Cerrig	rock/rocks	Mawr (Fawr)	great
Cefn	back of	Moel	mountain with grassy top
Ceunant	ravine	Mynedd	mountain
Coch (Goch)	red	Nant	valley
Coed	forest	Ogof	cave
Clogwyn	precipice, cliff	Pant	hollow
Craegiau	rocks	Pen	summit, top or head
Craig	rock	Pentre	village
Crib	ridge	Plas	hall
Cribin	ridge	Pont	bridge
Cwm	deep rounded hollow, corrie	Porth	bay
Dol	meadow	Rhaiadr	waterfall
Du (ddu)	black	Rhiw (iau)	steep place
Dwr	water	Sarn	stepping stones
Eglwys	Church	Tal	towering
Fford	road	Traeth	shore
Ffridd	cleared area, wood	Trwyn	promontory
Ffynnon	source of	Twll	hole
Foel	mountain	Ty	house
Ffrwd, Rhyd	ford	Uchaf	upper
		Wen (f)	white
Gallt (allt)	slope, ascent	Ynys	island

Appendix V
OPEN SEASON FOR FISHING IN WELSH RIVERS
These dates - accurate for 1985 - are subject to minor changes.

		JAN	FEB	MAR	APR	MAY	JUN	JUL	AUG	SEP	OCT	NOV	DEC
SALMON	Gwynedd			20th ◀						▶	17th		
	W. Wales			20th ◀						▶	17th		
	Gower			20th ◀						▶	17th		
	Taff			20th ◀						▶	17th		
	Usk	26th ◀								▶	17th		
	Dee & Clwyd	26th ◀ ─── R. DEE & TRIBUTARIES ─── ▶ 17th											
				20th ◀ - R. CLWYD & TRIBUTARIES ── ▶ 17th									
	Wye	26th ◀ -- R. WYE BELOW LLANWRTHWL BRIDGE ·-▶ 17th											
		26th ◀─ R. WYE ABOVE LLANWRTHWL BRIDGE- ▶ 25th											
	Wye	26th ◀─── ALL TRIBUTARIES OF R. WYE · ─── ▶ 25th											
SEA TROUT				20th ◀ · ALL WATERS - ALL DIVISIONS ▶ 17th									
BROWN TROUT				3rd ◀ BROWN TROUT IN RIVERS ▶ 30th (ALL DIVISIONS)									
				BROWN TROUT 31st ◀ (lower reaches) ▶ 30th (ALL DIVISIONS EXCEPT WYE)									
				20th ◀ BROWN TROUT IN STILL WATERS ▶ 17th (ALL DIVISIONS)									
				3rd ◀─── EGLWYS NUNYDD ───▶ 30th									
		15th ◀─── BROWN TROUT LLYN TEGID (BALA) ───▶ 14th											
		1st ◀ BROWN TROUT LLYN TRAWSFYNYDD ─▶ 31st											
RAINBOW TROUT				3rd ◀ RAINBOW TROUT IN RIVERS ▶ 30th									
		◀── RAINBOW TROUT IN STILL WATERS (NO CLOSE SEASON) ──▶											
FRESH WATER FISH			▶14th		16th ◀							
		ALL DIVISIONS WITH THE EXCEPTION OF GWYNEDD											
		◀── GWYNEDD DIVISION - NO CLOSE SEASON ──▶											
EELS		USK (BELOW GEORGE STREET, NEWPORT) DEE & CLWYD/GWYNEDD WYE DIVISIONS - NO CLOSE SEASON											
				▶14th		16th ◀						
		(WEST WALES/GOWER/TAFF & REMAINING USK DIVISION)											

OPEN SEASON SHOWN ◀─────────▶
YOU MAY FISH ON AND BETWEEN THE DATES SHOWN

Appendix VI

CARTOGRAPHY AND BIBLIOGRAPHY

MAPS

The Guide Book Maps are not sufficient in themselves for the river or sea canoeist. They lack detail and they lack precision. They are intended only to be quick visual guides to the trips. So the relevant Ordnance Survey Maps are an indispensible asset to canoeists.

The most readily available and useful maps are the 1:50,000 series. There are 203 of these covering England, Scotland and Wales; but, don't panic, for the trips described here (excluding The Severn Bore), you only need, at the most, 7. Just 3 in fact - Caernarfon & Bangor, Anglesey, and Lleyn Peninsular - cover the vast majority. Listed below are the appropriate *1:50,000 Ordnance Survey Maps* for each river, sea trip, and surf beach in the Guide.

Map Title: Anglesey
Sheet No: 114
Guide Book Reference:
　　Llandwyn Island, Newborough Warren, Cable Bay, Rhosneigr, Rhoscolyn, Penrhyn Mawr, The Stacks, Holy Island, Sandy Beach Farm, The Skerries, Anglesey-North Coast, Bull Bay, Anglesey-East Coast, Traeth Llugwy, Puffin Island, The Menai Strait.

Map Title: Caernarfon & Bangor
Sheet No: 115
Guide Book Reference:
　　The Menai Strait, Puffin Island, The Ormes, The Ogwen, The Seiont, The Colywn, The Glaslyn, The Llugwy, The Nantygwyrd, The Nantmor, The Lledr, The Gwyrfai.

Map Title: Denbigh & Colwyn Bay
Sheet No: 116
Guide Book Reference:
　　The Conwy, The Ormes.

Map Title: Chester
Sheet No: 117
Guide Book Reference:
　　The Lower Dee, The Dee Bore.

Map Title: Lleyn Peninsula
Sheet No: 123
Guide Book Reference:
　　The Tudwals, Porth Ceiriad, Hell's 'Mouth, Aberdaron, Bardsey, Lleyn Peninsular-North Coast, Dinas Dinlle.

Map Title: Dolgellau
Sheet No: 124
Guide Book Reference:
> The Artro, The Eden and Mawddach, The Wnion, Black Rock
> Sands.

Map Title: Bala & Lake Vyrnwy
Sheet No: 125
Guide Book Reference:
> The Tryweryn, The Upper Dee

Charts

In addition to Ordnance Survey Maps, the sea canoeist will find
Admiralty Charts an important source of information. In the 1:75,000
series only 3 are needed; the 1:25,000 scale is somewhat detailed for all
except the chart worm. Listed below are relevant *Admiralty Charts*
for the Guide Book area.

Chart No. 1413   *Approaches to Holyhead Harbour*, Scale 1:25,000.
                 Metric 1976.

Chart No. 1464   *The Menai Strait*, Scale 1:25,000, Metric 1975.

Chart No. 1977   *Holyhead to Great Ormes Head*, Scale 1:75,000,
                 Metric 1976.

Chart No. 1970   *Caernarvon Bay*, Scale 1:75,000, Metric 1976.

Chart No. 1971   *Cardigan Bay, Northern Part*, Scale 1:75,000,
                 Metric 1975.

Books

While most of the information in this Guide has not previously appeared in print, there were several important written sources. *North Wales White Water*, which I wrote with Jim Hargreaves in 1980, is the basis for many of the river descriptions, although there is much new material in this Guide. Robert Kemp's *Cruising Guide* to Anglesey was both a source of historical knowledge, and tidal information, and it is to him that I owe my understanding of the tidal streams in the Menai Strait. While Kemp sailed in, and wrote for, yachts, Glazebrook explored the coast in a dinghy, and his *Pilot* therefore, has more of the detail that a sea canoeist needs. Unfortunately, this mine of information on tides and inshore passages is now out of print, and hard to find. Laver's *Liverpool Tide Tables*, Reed's *Nautical Almanac*, and the *Admiralty Pilot*, were important sources of factual information. A bibliography is given below:

North Wales White Water; by Terry Storry & Jim Hargreaves; Cascade Press; 1980.

A Cruising Guide to Anglesey and the Menai Strait; by Robert Kemp; James Laver Printing Co. Ltd. 1977.

Anglesey and North Wales Coast Pilot; by F.H.Glazebrook, revised by Norman Sheldrick; Yachting Monthly; third edition 1970; now O.P.

Laver's Liverpool Tide Table 1985; James Laver Printing Co. Ltd., published each year.

Reed's Nautical Almanac 1985; Thomas Reed Publications Ltd., published every year.

Admiralty Pilot for the West Coasts of England and Wales; Hydographer of the Navy; 1974.

Printed by Carnmor Print & Design,
95/97, London Road, Preston, Lancashire.